THE ENCYCLOPEDIA OF WEALTH BUILDING OPPORTUNITIES

MONEY MANUAL NO. 1—REAL ESTATE WEALTH BUILDING OPPORTUNITIES
How To Buy And Sell Real Estate
For Maximum Profits

MONEY MANUAL NO 2—INVESTMENT OPPORTUNITIES FOR THE MID 1980'S
Wealth Building Strategies In The Stock Market,
Gold, Silver, Diamonds...

MONEY MANUAL NO. 3—SECRETS OF THE MILLIONAIRES
How The Rich Made It Big

MONEY MANUAL NO. 4—THE DYNAMICS OF PERSONAL FINANCIAL PLANNING
How To Save, Invest, And Multiply Your Money.

MONEY MANUAL NO. 5—HOW TO START MAKING MONEY IN A BUSINESS OF YOUR OWN
A Guide To Money Making Opportunities

MONEY MANUAL NO. 6—A TREASURY OF HOME BUSINESS OPPORTUNITIES
How to Make Money Without Leaving Home.

MONEY MANUAL NO. 7—HOW TO ACHIEVE TOTAL SUCCESS
How To Use The Power Of Creative Thought

Secrets of the Millionaires

How the Rich Made it Big

The do-it yourself millionaire kit

Published by:
George Sterne
Profit Ideas
8361 Vickers, Suite 304
San Diego, CA 92111

First edition—1984
First printing—1984
Second printing—1985
First soft cover edition—1987

Profit Ideas
8361 Vickers, Suite 304
San Diego, CA 92111

ISBN: 0-940398-20-6

ACKNOWLEDGMENTS

The publishers wish to express thanks to Jackson Fink for his contribution of research and writing to this book.

Secrets of the Millionaires
How The Rich Made It Big

Table of Contents

Chapter One

Making Your Dollars Work For You
How Interest Can Compound Your Money

"Wealth, viewed in its proper sense, is a means of increasing one's own creativity, a phase in the evolution of the human race."

Leonard Reed

If you set aside one dollar today, and squirrelled it away in a savings account that paid 5% simple interest, and if you saw to it that your account was updated each year, your family would have one million dollars by the year 2262.

Your family would be billionaires by the year 2403; and would be as wealthy as the combined fortunes of the Rockefellers, Rothschilds, DuPonts, and Mellons by the year 2453. You would be a trillionaire by the year 2544.

If the average price of land goes for $10,000 an acre, you could buy the state of Texas the following year - in 2545.

By 2667, you could buy every square inch of North America. And you could own all the earth's land area by 2703.

You would have enough capital by 2883 to earn twice as many dollars in annual interest as the number of inches traveled by a beam of light for one full year. And only 48 years later - in 2931 - you could be earning **ten times** as much money!

And in the year 2992, you would earn as much money in interest as the total principal you had in 2931!

Coming back to earth for a moment, it is important to see why this marvelous gift of compound interest is available for everyone to use.

There is much more than empty space behind the old expression, "time is money". The march of time is pervasive - and it can't be stopped by breaking the hands off a clock, interrupting the sway of a pendulum, standing in the way of a sun dial, setting back your watch, or tearing the pages off a calendar.

Time is the scarcest resource that a man has to work with. Each second is unique - it only passes by once, and life is short. Living life to its fullest means getting as much done as soon as possible.

The rational individual prefers having a dollar today to having that same dollar later. A dollar today is valued more highly than a dollar one year from now. The sooner an individual has his money, the sooner he can spend it on the things he wants, or the sooner he can tuck it into a savings account or an investment program and start earning interest. The longer he has to wait for his money, the less he values it. It costs him money to wait.

Money has time value. An individual won't loan a dollar unless he can get back more than a dollar at some future date. Why should anyone loan money and put off buying the things he wants, unless he has a reason? Interest is that reason.

Man reflects his time preference through interest rates. If he is anxious to spend his money, he will demand a higher interest rate. If he isn't too concerned about buying things right away, he is willing to take less interest on his loans and investments. Interest rates guide the employment of money along channels that are sensitive to the passage of time. All investment decisions are sensitive to interest rates, and the change in overall interest rates are known to have profound effects on the economy.

Interest is as natural as the law of gravity. Clearly, you can't keep compounding your money forever into space, nor will your family be masters of the globe in 725 years.

But you can be sure of one thing; through careful financial planning, you can use compound interest to become a millionaire several times over - and you can do it in your life time.

NOTES

Chapter Two

Turning Pennies into Dollars

"Everything I do, I do for a profit."

H.L. Hunt

If you were to buy one ounce of gold, and if you lent it to people who paid you back 5% interest - in gold - your family would own all the gold in the world by the year 2406.

This isn't so incredible when you stop to think that had this idea occured to one of the Spanish foot soldiers who conquered Mexico, that foot soldier's family would have had title to all the world's gold by 1948!

If one of the pilgrims had set aside one dime in a 6% bank account, his descendants would now have an estate valued at $108 million.

If the Indians who sold Manhattan to the Dutch for $24 had placed that money into a 6% savings account at the Bank of England, they would now have close to $20 billion - which is more than the current value of Manhattan!

Or if a Hebrew boy had found a gerah (1/20 of a shekel, or 2¾¢) at the time Christ was born, and put in the bank to draw a skimpy 1% interest, his estate would now be valued at $8.8 million.

And if you were to begin with one penny at the start of the month, and double it each day, you would have over 10½ million dollars by the time the 31st day of the month rolled around.

The moral behind these examples is that ever since the dawn of time, the real opportunities have been missed by billions and billions of people. The really sad story is that **any person** could have made a fortune.

Had General Washington invested $14,500 in 1789 at 10%,

there would have accumulated enough money to completely wipe out today's national debt!

Simple financial planning would have raised any number of unknown people to the level of wealth, stature, notoriety, and prestige currently enjoyed by the Rockefellers of the world.

To take a fictional, though plausible example, let's take a look at the financial journeys of seven brothers over their working lives.

All of them drop out of high school to become day laborers. They marry right away and start building their families early in life.

They only earn $2.50 an hour - that's just $5,000 per year. They live modestly, pay their bills on time, and set aside 10% each year for saving.

An intellectual pundit might smirk at the notion of day laborers who are "blighted by fate" of ever achieving financial success. They might muse, "An individual can only build a fortune if he is already earning fifteen or twenty thousand dollars a year."

Nothing could be further from the truth. You don't have to save much, it doesn't require a prodigious interest rate, and you don't need a whole lot of luck to make a fortune - if you have a plan.

Some may agree and say that although this might be true, it could take hundreds of years - long after our day laborer is dead.

This statement is not ground in reality. Just $500 sequestered away each year in a savings program can do some amazing things.

Let's take a look at the first laboring brother, Slim. Just like the others, Slim is very cautious. He saves 10% of his paycheck each year, and puts his $500 savings into the bank, drawing 6% interest.

16

Slim is satisfied. By the time he is 40, he has $22,000 in his account. He decides to stop saving anymore money out of his pay check, and just let the interest accumulate on the money he has already stashed away.

Slim retires at age 65 - with a $95,000 passbook balance. He lives off the interest in his account, and can spend $700 more each year than he could when he was working!

Slim's brother, Jim, also starts saving when he is 18 years old. Like Slim, he faithfully tucks away $500 each year until he reaches 40. Then he stops saving, and leaves his money alone to multiply by itself. But Jim doesn't put his money in the bank. Instead, he invests in things like trust deeds and bonds. It isn't hard for Jim to get a 10% return on his money.

Jim has $37,000 when he stops saving at 40. He is able to retire at 65 on a $400,000 bank roll earning him $40,000 a year!

Tim follows in his brothers' footsteps, but Tim devotes a significant amount of time and effort making sure his money earns as much as it possibly can. Tim gets a 12% return - something that is fairly easily attainable with enough search and diligence.

Tim has set aside $11,000 of his wages by the time he stops saving at 40 - but has $49,000 worth of investments! He retires on $833,000 of saved capital that returns him a yield of $100,000 each year.

Brother Kim gets a 15% return on his investments. He has $74,000 when he stops saving at age 40. Interest compounded on top of interest allows Kim to retire with a $2.4 million bankroll giving him $365,000 each year. That's 1,000 a day for saving $11,000 over a period of 22 years!

But the fifth brother, Gil, is somewhat lucky. He was able to get 20% each year on his investments. He has almost $150,000 when he stops saving at 40, and retires with a $14.2 million figure posted on the ledgers. Gil lives the rest of his days off the $2.8 million dollars he now earns each year.

The sixth brother, Mil, is quite lucky, and draws a 25% return on his money. He is worth $300,000 by the time he hits 40, and is worth $80 million when he retires. Mil can keep his money intact, and spend $20 million **each year.**

Brother Bill is the luckiest brother of them all (that's why he was the seventh). Bill has quite a flair for investing his money - and he pulls an unbelievable 50% return each year. He has over $9 million by the time he is 40, and retires with $236 billion - more than the combined fortunes of the world's five wealthiest families!

So even over a single lifetime, a person of modest means can accumulate a more than comfortable nest egg without too much trouble. An investor doesn't have to be born with a silver spoon in his mouth either, to become a man of great wealth. And although Bill's 50% return and Mil's 25% are fun to dream about, and not something to count on, returns between 10 and 20 percent are within the grasp of every breathing American.

If a day laborer Gil could accumulate 14 million dollars, so can you!

NOTES

Chapter Three

GETTING TO KNOW THE
FINANCIAL YOU

"Life, faculties, production - in other words individuality, liberty, property - this is man."

Frederic Bastiat

Before a person can even take the first step toward making a fortune, he must know about himself as an investor. The investor should take a personality inventory of his strength and weaknesses. He must know what he is capable of doing, and understand the character traits underlying his personal hopes and ambitions. Only then can he have a better handle on his decision-making processes.

Before he can even start, the investor must come to task with where he stands at the present time. Before trying to chart a path, design a plan, or determine a course of action, he must first know the location and dimensions of the starting point.

Without question, the most important question that must be answered is "how much money must I make to be satisfied with myself"?

As mentioned before, every person has an internal, personal, natural interest rate, reflecting his time preference valuations. Finding your own natural resonant interest rate is the same thing as finding how big a return you need to be satisfied with your achievements.

The investor who is paid a sum of money at some later date is put in the position of deferring the options that are available to him. The rational investor demands a **premium** on money that is paid to him in the future.

The premium on deferred money payments is called interest. And interest is as natural as the laws of supply and demand.

But what do interest payments have to do with personal investor psychology? Plenty. Because every investor has a different anxiety level toward deferred payment.

Some investors don't care as much about deferred payments as other investors do. They demand less of a premium on the money they loan. They are satisfied with receiving less interest on their loans.

Other investors place a very high value on getting paid right away. They will take their money later, but only if they get a higher premium.

These people must receive higher interest rates to be satisfied. Economists would say that money for these people has a high time value.

Each investor values time differently. This valuation is tied in with his character. Whether he has a high time valuation, and demands higher interest rates, or whether he has a low time valuation and accepts lower interest rates is not important. Both kinds of people have become millionaires. And before you can become one, you should know what kind of person you are.

There are three personal inventories that can be used to help you become familiar with your personal investment characteristics and traits.

Please do not skip these tests. It is important that you take each one.

I. FIRST INVESTOR INVENTORY EXAMINATION

You are presented with four investment opportunities;

Rank these opportunities in the order from best to worst.
  (A) $2,000 in 2 years
  (B) $3,000 in 5 years
  (C) $4,500 in 10 years
  (D) $1,000 in 2 years and $2,000 in 5 years.
Put Your Personal Ranking Here: _A D B C_____
This is your answer to the first test.

II. SECOND INVESTOR INVENTORY EXAMINATION

How long would you be willing to wait to double your money?
Put your answer here: _2 yrs_____

What's the **longest** period of time you would be willing to wait to double your money? Put your answer here: _2 yr__

Put down your last answer again:_2 yrs._____

This is your answer to the second test.

III. THIRD INVESTOR INVENTORY EXAMINATION

How much would you put into an investment that would be worth $10,000 in two years? Put your answer here: _2500_

What's the **most** you would be willing to put into that investment?
Put your answer here: ___2500_____
Put down your last answer again:___2500_____

This is your answer to the third test.

Analyzing the Results

TEST I.

If you ranked the investment opportunities in the order CABA, your personal time preference interest rate is around 6%.

If you ranked the investment opportunities in the order DCBA, your personal time preference rate is around 7%.

If you ranked the investment opportunities in the order DBAC, your personal time preference rate is around 13%.

If you ranked the investment opportunities in the order DABC, your personal time preference rate is around 20%.

If you ranked the investment opportunities in the order ADBC, your personal time preference rate is around 50% ✓

WRITE DOWN YOUR PERSONAL TIME PREFERENCE RATE OF RETURN: _50 %_

TEST II.

Write down your answer to the second test: _5 yrs_

If that answer is about 1 years, your personal investment rate of return is about 100 percent.

(2)	(41)
3	26
4	21
5	17
6	13
7	11
8	9
9	8
10	7
11	6

WRITE DOWN THE PERCENTAGE SHOWN IN THE CHART: _41%_

This is your personal investment rate of return.

Write down your answer to the third test: _2500_

Divide that answer into $10,000. Write down this figure. (It should be bigger than 1): _4_

Take the square root of that figure: Write down the answer _2_

Subtract 1 from that answer, and write down the number: _1_

Multiply this number by 100. Put the solution here: _100_

WRITE DOWN THIS SOLUTION AGAIN: _100_

This is your average private rate of return.

23

What to do With These Numbers

Write down your personal time preference rate of return: 2

Write down your personal investment rate of return: 41

Write down your average private rate of return: 100

Pick the two numbers that are closest together. Add these two numbers together, and write down the sum: 43

Divide the sum by 2. Write it down: 21.5

WRITE DOWN THIS FINAL NUMBER AGAIN: 21.5

This number is your approximate resonant interest rate. It is not exact, but chance are pretty good, on the average, that your own personal interest rate is approximately at this level.

Your resonant interest rate expresses your time preference rating. This is the rate that makes you content. This is the minimum return that you should shoot for getting on your money each year. Your character traits suggest that you will be dissatisfied getting a smaller return on your money.

Now that you know your own private interest rate, you can make some interesting comparisons.

Look at the example of a man starting a savings program at age 30, and retiring at 65:

24

Interest Rate	Amount of money he would have if he let $10,000 compound until he reached retirement	Amount he would have to invest to have a million dollars when he retires	Years it takes for a $10,000 investment to reach one million dollars
5 percent	$ 55,210	$181,100	94
6 percent	76,810	130,200	79
7 percent	106,900	93,540	68
8 percent	147,600	67,770	60
9 percent	203,700	49,090	54
10 percent	281,200	35,570	49
11 percent	385,000	25,970	44
12 percent	527,200	18,965	41
13 percent	722,000	13,850	38
14 percent	900,600	10,200	35
15 percent	1,332,000	7,509	33
16 percent	1,809,000	5,528	31
17 percent	3,284,500	3,044	28
18 percent	4,390,000	2,278	27
19 percent	5,915,000	1,690	25
20 percent	7,908,000	1,265	24
21 percent	10,055,000	947	23
22 percent	14,110,000	714	22
24 percent	18,580,000	539	21
25 percent	24,635,000	406	21
33⅓ percent	235,200,000	43	16

NOTES

Chapter Four

THE CAPTAINS OF BUSINESS

"Example is the school of mankind; they learn at no other."

Edmund Burke

The universities are filled with intelligent paupers. Many highly esteemed professors of economics lose thousands of dollars each year in the course of "investing" their money.

The DuPonts, on the other hand, were refugees from France. Andrew Carnegie's father was a poor Scotch immigrant. Rockefeller was a dry goods clerk. And Edward Harriman was the office boy in a brokerage house.

Why can't learned scholars successfully use the knowledge they have been taught, while seemingly unsophisticated novices have a penchant for striking it rich?

Like the lessons of life, the techniques for becoming rich can't be taught in the class room. Wealth is acquired by those who are motivated by desire, and willing to work hard for what they want.

To become rich oneself, an individual might get some help by emulating the example of others who have been successful. And no example is better than that of steel magnate Andrew Carnegie.

Andrew Carnegie was just a 13 year old boy when he came to America in 1848. He was penniless, and worked as a bobbin boy for $1.20 a week to help support his family. In a year, he was a stoker and by the time he was 15, young Carnegie was earning $3 a week as a telegraph operator. He was pulling down $6 per week with the Pennsylvania Railroad by the time he was 19.

Then came Carnegie's first major break. He became the

private secretary to the railroad's Pittsburgh superintendant.

His new boss, Colonel Scott, was at the hub of information concerning every new business venture that was brewing in Pittsburgh. On a tip from his boss, combined with some daring of his own, young Carnegie made his first investment -without putting up one penny of his own money.

Carnegie bought an interest in a small Pennsylvania oil company with a note that was paid off in just one year from the stock's dividends. The proceeds of this venture became the seed money Carnegie used to speculate on local Pittsburgh stocks recommended by Colonel Scott.

For ten years, Carnegie remained Scott's secretary. And in 1864, at the age of 28, he replaced Scott as superintendant of the Railroad. That was also the year he invested $8,920 for a 17% interest in the Iron City Forge Company.

As superintendant for the railroad, Carnegie knew that iron was too soft for railroad rails. He knew that steel was more durable, he knew about the Bessemer process, he knew steel was too expensive, and he knew that iron was being smelted in small furnaces.

1864 was quite a prosperous year. Plans for Western railroads were being drawn up. The demand for iron rails was so high every iron plant, including the Iron City Forge Company, was operating at peak capacity.

This allowed the unit costs to fall, and the inexpensive manufacturing of steel began to approach real possibilities. Carnegie saw this, and so did the larger investment community. But Carnegie continued to manufacture iron, and formed the Keystone Bridge Company. Once again, he paid for this venture with a note, which was paid off in just four years from profits of the company.

It seems the Pennsylvania Railroad needed iron bridges at the time, and Carnegie saw to it that the Keystone Bridge Company received all the orders it could handle for iron bridges.

A recession set in when the civil war ended. Carnegie made the best of a bad set of circumstances. By the time the turnaround came, Andrew Carnegie emerged the sole owner of the Iron City Forge company. By 1873 Andrew Carnegie was a multimillionaire on the way to becoming the King of Steel.

Andrew Carnegie was not a pioneer in the steel industry. He entered the business only after others had already demonstrated its profitability. He invested on the basis of leads and inside information, and often used other people's money to do it.

Carnegie made full use of his position for personal benefit, as demonstrated by the Keystone Bridge Company. He always had his eyes open looking at every new set of conditions from the perspective of how he could make money from it. He saw everything in a financial light. He filtered events; focused and processed them with one central theme in mind -"how can I use this opportunity to advance myself."

Carnegie became a stoker because he was a good bobbin boy. He saw the opportunity behind becoming a telegraph operator for a railroad because it paid better. He saw the chance to learn about venture finance by watching the Pittsburgh railroad superintendent in action, as his personal secretary for ten years.

John D. Rockefeller was in many ways like Andrew Carnegie. He began his career as a clerk in Cleveland. He assiduously saved $700 and, in 1860 went drilling for petroleum with three other men. By 1862, the firm was worth $4000, and was getting most of its business from refining operations.

Rockefeller always kept large cash reserves, because he was never quite sure whether or not the supply of oil would run out. The Standard Oil Company of Ohio was formed in 1870, with $1 million in assets and no liabilities. Fiscal solvency

29

turned out to be a prime asset for all firms starting out in 1870, because a recession struck that year and many debt-ridden refiners were besieged with trouble. Banks kept away from the precarious oil industry as a general rule, and they certainly didn't want to make loans to debt-ridden refiners floundering in the midst of a recession.

So the shaky companies sold out to Standard Oil, and handed Standard its opportunity to become a national operation. Standard had $13 million in cash reserves by 1875, and was refining on such large scale that it was producing at a much lower unit cost than any other competitor.

This advantage was used to both bargain transport rates with the railroads as well as rebates, at the expense of small less efficient refiners. Soon Standard was buying pipelines and laying their own pipe. By 1879, they were a monopoly with 90% of the business. In 1881, Standard Oil had $45 million in cash reserves.

Several traits should be singled out when analyzing Rockefeller. Like Carnegie, Rockefeller had an intensely acquisitive character. He was circumspect, but not overly cautious. When Rockefeller reached a decision, he focused all his available energies on implementing a successful outcome. He was both a planner and a doer.

Rockefeller was always on the prowl for new business opportunities. This may be one reason why he tried to stay as liquid as possible. At the same time, Rockefeller was an audacious plunger, sinking his entire savings of $700, for example, into a small oil exploration firm. Rockefeller saved his money and kept it working all the time.

Edward Harriman was born the son of a poor minister in 1848. He went to work as an office boy in a brokerage firm when he was just 14 years old. Like Carnegie, Harriman saved his money and used his savings on stock speculations. He bought himself a seat on the New York Stock Exchange when he was 22 - when he was just a bookkeeper. Harriman started a brokerage partnership and dissolved it after enough money was earned to go into business for himself.

By the time he was 32, he had accumulated $300,000 from trading and brokering stock. He worked his way into a seat on the Board of Directors of the Illinois Central Railroad. He bought part of the Wabash, Saint Louis, and Pacific after it dissolved in 1884. He bought part of the Dubuque and Sioux City Railroad in 1887. He bought an important section of the Saint Louis, Alton, and Terre Haute, and purchased roadbed that pinched off the Southern Pacific from the Atlantic.

At the age of 39, Edward Harriman controlled the major arteries of commerce in America. From 2,000 miles of road-bed in 1883, Harriman controlled a 5,000 mile system by 1897. He re-organized the great Union-Pacific Railroad and became Chairman of the Board.

Harriman's chief character trait was the goal-oriented aura of determination and purpose. Harriman was always searching for ways to make money; first in the brokerage business (because that's where he worked as a boy) and later with railroads. Like Carnegie, it probably didn't matter much to Harriman what kind of business he got into. He was an entrepreneur; a capitalist; a manager. Carnegie knew very little about the technical process of making steel and likewise Harriman had complete familiarity with only the managerial/financial side of the railroads.

The financial empire of J.P. Morgan started out as a small dry goods business.

In 1811, a 16 year old dry goods clerk named George Peabody worked in a dry goods store owned by his brother in Newbury, Massachusetts. The store burnt down and finding himself unemployed, a young Peabody traveled to Washington D.C. But unlike many people today, who go to our nation's capital in search of a hand-out, or subsidies, Peabody went there to open a small retail dry goods store. He started his own business.

By the time George Peabody was 42, there were branches in Philadelphia and New York. The merchant banking house of George Peabody & Company was then formed.

George Peabody was competing with international giants like the Rothchilds when he retired at 69. The firm was passed on to another dry good dealer named Junius S. Morgan - who was a member of the Boston dry good firm of J.M. Beebe & Company.

The name of the new firm was changed to J.S. Morgan & Company only shortly after Peabody's death. And J.S. Morgan & Company became the fiscal launching pad to be used by a young J.P. Morgan in his catapult to supremacy over a multi-billion dollar banking empire.

The rise of the Vanderbilt family started with the birth of Cornelius Vanderbilt in 1794. He started working at 16 by running a small boat that carried vegetables and passengers into New York City. By the time he was 23, he already had amassed $10,000 in savings.

Vanderbilt started a steamship line, which he sold at the end of the civil war to transfer his capital into railway stocks. Over the course of his life, Cornelius Vanderbilt secured control over a number of railroads which he consolidated into the New York Central and Hudson River Railroad. At the time of his death, Cornelius Vanderbilt owned over 2,000 miles of track.

His son, William Henry Vanderbilt, developed the Vanderbilt system of railroads by affiliating both the New York Central and Hudson River Railroads with important western railways such as the Michigan Southern; Lake Shore; and the Chicago and Northwestern Railroads.

The famous Hearst publishing chain actually started out as a mining company. George Hearst was a miner who accumulated a fortune tunneling under the earth, first for a salary and later for himself - when he formed his own company. In his dealings, George Hearst acquired a newspaper called the San Francisco Examiner, and his son, William Randolph, forged, from that keystone, a veritable chain of newspapers in key cities throughout America. He multiplied the money left him by his father over ten times, and died one of the most powerful men in America.

J.P. Morgan, the Vanderbilts, and the Hearsts built their financial empires over the span of generations. There was no industrial continuity at the times these families were accumulating great stores of wealth. Financier Morgan knew little about the dry goods business, except that it lifted him to the position of banker. The later Vanderbilts seldom gave even a second thought to ocean steamers. The Hearst's world of publishing is in no way even remotely connected to mines.

The captains of business followed one simple rule - follow the line of profit. They were always vigilant and on the lookout for new profit possibilities. And when they recognized these opportunities, it mattered little what the specific industry or business was. All that mattered was how to pull money out of a set of economic conditions.

NOTES

Chapter Five

TODAY'S MILLIONAIRES

"In the free market one gains wealth only through serving the consumers best, as determined by the opinion of those very consumers themselves."

John Hospers

Andrew Carnegie was the king of steel for the same reason Rockefeller was an oil magnate for the same reason Harriman was a railroad giant. Each man recognized the opportunities for profit that existed in their industries, and rushed to meet the needs of the market place.

The successful businessman properly interprets the demands of the consumers, and understands what he can do to serve the wants he sees expressed in the de-centralized mechanism of the free market place. Those who best serve the wants of the consumers are well rewarded for their accomplishments.

Carnegie invested in oil, iron, and bridges before he manufactured steel. He worked in textiles, telegraph communications, and railroads before dabbling with the practical applications of the Bessemer process.

Rockefeller was a dry goods clerk before cutting his eye teeth on the oil industry.

These examples are poised in direct opposition to the frequent chants uttered by most common people today; namely that, "the age of the industrial revolution is long since past. The days of up and coming billionaires are gone. There is no way another Carnegie or Rockefeller can make it on his own. In these modern times, it is more difficult than ever to make a million dollars."

The age of opportunity is not dead. The only stagnation that exists is that which is pooled up inside the minds of these

35

negative thinkers.

Fortunes have been made in the past, fortunes are being made now, and fortunes will be made in the future. New people with new ideas and perceptive qualities will continually rise to financial prominence in the flux of changing market conditions. The presence of industrial giants in no way impedes the accumulation of new fortunes, or the growth of new firms.

Harriman, after all, built a railroad empire at the time Cornelius Vanderbilt was the undisputed leader of the industry. Morgan built a financial empire even though the larger, and better-financed Rothchilds wielded immense economic clout. Even the Rothchilds started their own banking dynasty in the presence of larger, established competitors.

Fifty years after Morgan grasped hold of the American banking monopoly, a San Francisco fruit peddler started on his way toward building the largest bank in the world - the Bank of America...

New innovators are always coming along. It doesn't take much to see how enormously different our life style is now, compared to just fifty years ago. Color T.V.'s, microwave ovens, mini-computers, well-designed cars, moon landings, robots conducting chemical analysis of the soil on Mars and Venus, Xerox machines, automatic typewriters, wonder drugs, heart surgery, electronic transmission of pictures,...

Just a generation ago, people marveled at moving pictures, radio, the "horseless carriage", the electric light bulb, airplanes, the telephone,...

People were just as amazed over the invention of the steam engine, the printing press, arabic numerals, and fire.

Wherever man has been free to think, society has been blessed with a few productive innovators. And salient individuals are stepping to the forefront every day, bringing good ideas and capitalizing on them to meet the demands in the market place. The new entrant with the new, better idea, who uses that idea to meet the wants of the consuming public can't help but slice away a share of the market for himself.

Innovators eventually get tired and old, or they die and pass their firm on to people who are less competent than themselves. This provides the opportunity for another more efficient individual to come along and cut away a share of the market. Consumers are only interested in better products and lower prices. The producer who best fills the consumer's wants will be the firm that the consumers patronize - no matter how small or large, new or established.

The whole process of the market place is centered around serving the consumers with the products and services they desire. Those firms who are successful at filling those wants are rewarded through customer sales. Competition ensures that those who best serve the public are rewarded with the highest profits. Those who succeed make profits, and expand. Those who don't serve the consuming public very well lose sales, lose money, and must contract.

The best always rise to the top in a free market.

Although Carnegie made a fortune in the steel industry, his firm today has less than a quarter of the market. The steel industry is falling apart, and facing heavy competition from Japanese producers - who were ravaged by war just thirty years ago.

Rockefeller once controlled 90 percent of the petroleum industry. Now, the largest oil company supplies 7% of the market.

The Penn-Central Railroad - once the largest company in America, a scion of mighty Vanderbilt, and the descendent of the firm Carneigie worked for to get positioned in the steel business - is now broke. Harriman built an empire off the rails; now they are in financial ruin.

The growth industries of yesterday are in trouble today. A

good choice of options many years ago would put today's producer in serious jeopardy.

Tastes change; processes change; the prominent individuals with nev ideas change; the consumers change; the same consumers are whimsical and capricious.

Today's market place is vastly more complex than it was thirty years ago. It will be far more complex in just ten more years.

The more uncertain, and the more complex the market, the better chance any individual has to recognize a product, service, or some combination of the two as a want the consumers would like to have satisfied - and are willing to pay for.

The more complex the society, the less successful will centralized agencies be with directing the affairs of individuals. The winner of the 1975 Nobel Prize in economics, Fredrich Von Hayek, likens this to a super-saturated solution that is almost at the point of precipitating a crystal. All it takes is a gentle tap on the side of the beaker, or slight decrease in temperature, or a tiny grain dropped inside to make one atom precipitate; triggering other atoms to precipitate too, by latching onto the sides of the microscopic crystal.

A **perfect** crystal grows in the flask. Without any outside direction individual atoms fuse together into an orderly structure.

Had the chemist shaken the flask, or dropped something else in, or tried "breaking apart" the developing crystal, the perfection would have been destroyed. Many times, complexity is better approached by approaching it from a decentralized angle.

The free market place is without doubt the best decentralized mechanism for both the many consumers and competing producers. Today's entrepreneur is **lucky** to live in an advanced society, with its multitude of opportunities.

It is far easier to make a million dollars today than it ever was. It required as much effort in 1914 to earn a million dollars as it now takes to make five million dollars. You can make a million today with less than 20 percent the effort it took sixty years ago.

There are an estimated 500,000-plus millionaires in the United States today—one in every 500 Americans is a millionaire.

The opportunities to become a millionaire are greater today than they have ever been.

One lady invested $100 when the Ford Motor Company was inside a garage; she got back $260,000 in capital gains and $95,000 in dividends.

Another individual gave Henry Ford $5,000 - and got back almost $17½ million.

Opportunities like Ford Motors don't come along every day, but it can't be said they no longer exist. Profits like these are quite possible in other places besides firms that are rising as leaders in a new industry.

Had you invested $1,000 in Polaroid forty years ago, that stock would now be worth over $4 million.

General Doriot acquired a 60% interest in an obscure company named Digital Equipment. Within eleven years, Doriot was worth 250 million dollars.

J.P. Getty inherited an estate worth $15 million. His 30% interest in the Getty Oil Company became the springboard for becoming not only a billionare - but the wealthiest man in America as well.

Howard Hughes turned the Hughes Tool Company into a billion dollar conglomerate; William Randolph Hearst turned a mining company into a powerful and expansive newspaper chain.

Hugh Roy Cullen, born in 1881 and died in 1957, was the son of a cattle man, and went to work when he was 12. Cullen eventually became a cotton broker, and changed occupations to oil man. He died leaving an estate valued at around $200 million.

Amadeo P. Giannini was the first fruit peddler who first built Bank of America into the world's largest bank and then put together the Transamerica Corporation.

William H. Danforth borrowed $4,000 from his father and went into the horse feed business with two other men in 1894, after graduating from Washington University. The Robinson-Danforth Commission Company set up the Purina Horsefeed division, with Bill Danforth handling sales. He owned ⅔ of the firm 2 years later, and the line was broadened to include other animal feeds. The "checkerboard squares" division was set up to market whole wheat cereals.

The depression hit and William Danforth handed over the crippled company to his son, Donald. Ralston-Purina grew under his management from an insignificant 19 million dollar feed company in 1932, into a 400 million dollar giant by 1956 - number 87 on the Fortune 500.

James A. Ryder was a day laborer in 1935. He now hauls freight and leases equipment through his firm, Ryder Systems, Inc. James Ryder is currently worth between ten and fifteen million dollars.

Winston J. Schuler only had $50,000 in 1946, but he bought a second rate restaurant, fixed it up, added a bowling alley, and generated the publicity necessary to make it popular. Winston Schuler is now the head of a 3 million dollar restaurant chain.

Robert Peterson was the son of an immigrant mechanic. He was a struggling California press agent when he started Hot Rod magazine. He is now worth 3 million dollars.

Thomas F. Bolack was the oil field day laborer who bought San Juan Basin Oil leases for 25¢ and acre and sold them for $5,000 apiece.

Sam Wyly parlayed a $1,000 investment in University

Computing Corporation into a $300 million firm earning $8½ million a year.

Ralph E. Schneifer started the Diners Club when he was a $15,000 per year lawyer. In just 20 years, Diners Club was worth $20 million.

John McIntosh operated an Orange County, California snack bar in 1948. It has since grown into a chain of 135 restaurants including Reubens, Moonrakers, Baxter Street, Gorda Liz, and the Coco chains. His operation now stretches across the country and serves 100,000 people each day, and business is increasing steadily.

Sir Godfrey Mitchell bought the George Wimpey construction business inside socialist Britain in 1919 for $20,000. He retired with a $450 million nest egg.

Here are just a few examples of men who started a business in recent times, and were succesful in spite of the presence of firmly established giant corporations.

The Rockefellers or Mellons (each worth about 5 billion dollars) could do little to stand in the way of these kings of commerce.

The 8 billion dollar Du Pont fortune did not stop these men from making money. And the $100 billion dollars reputedly held by the Rothschilds has not lessened the enthusiasm of the 600 or more venture capital firms who do nothing else but look for and pump money into other people's projects.

In an economy dominated by giant corporations, it is inspirational to watch the dynamic processes of the market repeatedly knock down inefficient large-scale operations, and replace them with up and coming businesses who are outperforming the leaders. The criteria of efficiency and the changing flux of time gives every advantage to the new firm or individual who has the insight to recognize an opportunity and the motive, determination, and desire to act.

41

Large corporations lack flexibiltiy single individuals have. Large corporations are run by managers who are salaried and responsible for large budgets. By nature, they are careful, and slow to move. The cumbersome leader is less likely to notice and act upon opportunities that mean only a minor, risky, incremental profits. The quick, agile, mobile, new, alert, small scale entrepreneur can make a major financial incursion on the same opportunity.

The giant AT & T monopoly was once a small business in competition with the giant Western Union Telegraph Company. Ma Bell's one idea was a better way to communicate. She supplanted Western Union.

Henry Ford built and dominated the early auto industry. Ford motors is now number two - and has less than half the sales General Motors enjoys.

Underwood once dominated the office machine market. They nearly went broke, and are now the subsidiary of the Olivetti company - headquarters in Italy.

IBM has taken their place, and has assumed the number one spot in the computer business as well, edging out Burroughs and Sperry Rand.

But IBM, in turn, has spawned a great number of its own profitable spin offs. Max Pavlevsky's Scientific Data Systems, Ken Norris' Control Data Corporation, and Kenneth Olsen's Digital Equipment are a few.

Two highly succesful IBM offshoots are Ross Perot and Gene Amdahl.

Ross Perot was IBM's star salesman in Texas. It became embarrassing to IBM's management that a lowly salesman should be making more in commissions each year than the chairman of the Board.

So they slammed down a ceiling of $250,000 on the maximum allowable commission possible for any salesman to earn in any given year. Ross Perot earned his quota by the time January 31 rolled around.

What was he going to do? He wasn't going to sit on his hands for eleven months, and he sure wasn't going to work for free. So he quit, and started Electronic Data Services. By 1972, he was earning $16½ million each year and was worth $645 million.

Gene M. Amdahl designed the famous IBM series 360 computer. He became dissatisfied when IBM refused his proposal to introduce a new computer that could do more than current IBM computers, and could do it at a cheaper price.

It seemed Amdahl's invention would generate a profit margin smaller than that stipulated by IBM's top management. In addition, IBM feared that if the product was introduced, customers would shift toward it, since it had a higher productivity.

IBM's management envisioned scenes of sales cannabilism, where customers would substitute orders for the more highly productive unit, which would have generated a lower profit margin for IBM.

Amdahl resigned, and brashly warned the IBM leadership that he intended to compete with them, and go into business for himself.

Now Amdahl had no experience in business. He graduated from college with a PH.D. in physics, and had spent most of his college days designing the very first computer. He had no financial backing, no managerial experience, and a profound distaste for administrative policies of any kind.

IBM's management smirked, patted him on the back, wished him all the luck in the world, opened the door and told him he could come back any time he wished.

Two years, later the Amdahl Corporation was engineering sharp cuts into IBM sales. The IBM 168, which accounted for over a half billion dollars in computer sales, found that its volume was being sliced from the vigorous competition of

43

Amdahl's 470 V16.

The Amdahl 470 V16 did more for each customer dollar than did the IBM 168. It ran with IBM's peripheral equipment. As might be expected, Amdahl detached numerous former IBM clients from the computer giant. Bell Telephone, General Motors, and NASA lead the list.

Amdahl quit IBM in 1970. He raised $27½ million in venture capital by 1972. Part of it came from a Japanese computer manufacturer who was willing to loan money to Amdahl in exchange for a new source of technological development the Japanese firm needed to successfully compete with IBM. The second principal source of capital came from a venture capital firm, which was primarily interested in securing a good return on their money.

The Amdahl Corporation earned $92.8 million in gross revenue for the first year of operations, and posted a $24 million profit. Between $175 and $200 million were grossed in 1977, with roughly $50 million in profits.

So it isn't so hard after all to find a niche in the market that is crying to be filled.

A good idea turns opportunity into fortune. The real question is how to find that seed of fortune, and what to do with it once you have found it. The seed must be planted and nursed into a sapling. Only the skillful financial planner will properly care for its growth, and watch it mature into a full size tree - and maybe a forest.

There are many butchers chopping away on wooden blocks and earning a meager living; and then there is Raymond Bloye who carved out an 80 million dollar meat business for himself.

Asa Chandler, a back woods Georgia drug clerk, gave his life savings to a country doctor who was holding a charred black kettle of viscous ooze and a slip of paper containing the syrup's formula. Asa Chandler transformed his $500 investment into a soft drink that came to be named Coca-Cola.

The skillful entrepreneur can turn almost any circumstance into a seed for a growing sapling. A milk stand in Picadilly circus eventually grew into the Forte Hotels. Kelloggs cereals started out as a quest for a breakfast substitute. Honda Motors started out in a Tokyo garage.

These firms were different from all the rest. They took a good idea and coupled it with a plan. They had a firmly defined goal they were after, and were motivated to implement their plan through hard work. They re-invested, and used the laws of geometric progression to compound their investment over and over again. First there was one shop, plant, or facility. Then there were two, soon there were four, and then eight...

Carnegie did it. Rockefeller and Harriman did it. So did J.P. Morgan, Vanderbilt, and Hearst. The American dream was achieved by Ford, J.P. Getty, Howard Hughes, General Doriot, Hugh Cullen, A.P. Giannini, William Danforth, Jim Ryder, Winston Schuler, Robert Peterson, Thomas Bolack, Sam Wyly, Asa Chandler, Ralph Schneider, John McIntosh, Sir Godfrey Mitchell...

Why can't you do as well as some of them?

NOTES

Chapter Six

THE NUTS AND BOLTS

"The businessman, the acting man, is entirely absorbed in one task only; to take best advantage of all the means available for the improvement of future conditions."
Ludwig von Mises

Just **how** do they do it?

One way to find out is to look at the common traits shared by highly successful businessmen.

When this is done, one outstanding characteristic seems to pop up time and time again. This pervasive quality seems to be the entrepreneur's zeal for doing business and earning money. The zest comes not from the simple enjoyment of performing the individual business tasks, but rather from a deep felt urge, or internal drive. These men are driven to zealous performance because they have identified their work with the satisfaction of a deeply felt, programmed, urge to succeed.

This internal drive, is best conceptualized in the immigrants who have become successful in the new world. Andrew Carnegie and DuPonts are cases in point; both coming to America nearly broke, in search of any job that was offered to them. They needed money to eat. For them, working was a matter of survival.

The immigrant Carnegies used the money they earned to buy the essentials of life. And it took long hours of hard, menial work to buy the essentials. The immigrants valued their earnings much more than the less desperate domestic American valued his easily obtained pin money.

The successful immigrant, like every successful businessman, was driven to make money. He set goals, and had the fierce determination to reach them. In fact, it might be said that he lived his life for his goals. This added a spiritual dimension to his life - it added tang, purpose, and meaning to an otherwise dreary existence.

The desperate need to survive instilled a competitive nature in the immigrant. This burning drive was ingrained when he started out, and reinforced as he progressed. The immigrant's thrift permitted him to accumulate a small prized savings cache. A little bit is more than the immigrant had when he first came to America, and a modest savings was the symbol of success. Success to the struggling immigrant has ever so sweet a taste.

As things got better, the immigrant transformed the need to survive into the need to succeed. The successful man's life is spiced with the aroma of accomplishment when he is fiercely devoted to a goal that shows him a specific end; a goal which allows him to monitor the day to day progress toward that objective.

The successful immigrant demonstrates the importance of the alert, perceptive mind. Coming from a different culture, and thrust into a new country, he assimilates both experiences. As a result, the foreigner did not look at a situation with the same pair of eyes a native would. He was free of domestic preconceptions, prejudices, and thought processes. He didn't look at things the obvious way; he has what has been called "lateral thinking". The immigrant had a three dimensional mind.

In fact, the original willingness of the immigrants to do the work natives wouldn't do pushed them into non-established fields nobody else would touch such as chemicals and steel, later movies and electronics.

In every case, the successful business serves the consumer

in the market place by providing a product or service that is desired. The producer finds a want expressed by the market, and does his best to satisfy it. He looks for things consumers are willing to pay for. The producer often finds opportunity specifically where the rest of society does not wish to tread.

The producer slavishly meets the demands of the market place. He chooses the business he feels will make the most money, and provides the product or service the consumers most want. The producer is not in business to satisfy his own whims - he is serving the consumer where he expects a demand to exist.

The producer does **not** produce what he thinks the consumers **ought** to buy: to hope a demand might some day materialize. Rather, he knows he will reach his goal of fiscal advancement by serving the consumers and making money-properly interpreting and meeting the demands voiced by thousands of individuals in the market place.

The entrepreneur looks at everything from a fiscal vantage point, filtering everything he is exposed to through the financial center of his brain. The entrepreneur keeps his eyes open. He is always on the lookout for profitable possibilities.

In a way similar to the comparison between the immigrant and the domestic American, small producers have an intriguing advantage over the industrial corporate giants who make up a large part of the American economic machinery.

Small producers have a variegated first hand direct experience with the business. They are not as far removed from economic affairs as are the salaried corporate managers.

Neither is the small producer burdened with a sizeable managerial structure, or a stiff formal administrative policy. The corporate giants are less prone to take risks than are the small-scale independent entrepreneurs.

Big firms aren't nearly as flexible or agile as the smaller

businessmen who are more intuitive and mobile; personally and passionately involved with their work, in immediate public contact, their hand directly on the pulse of the market place. Chances are higher the small producer is obsessed with his job, and in a better position to recognize market changes much sooner than the statistical departments of larger firms.

The independent entrepreneur has the lateral capacity to seize upon a profit opportunity passed over, or missed by somnolent companies who are thoughtlessly bringing in easy profits.

Whether a chance comes from lower costs or a better product, service, or means of delivery, today's businessman can take advantage of the chinks in the armor of a dominant, but lazy, business or industry.

The successful producer doesn't take true risks. He is circumspect in his dealings. He may undertake a business deal others believe is risky, but he himself is sure will succeed. He only acts after he has watched others take the risks. He waits until he sees the mistakes other people make. He knows the draw backs and flaws; he knows what to do to correct them, and he has thorough understanding of the endeavor he is about to undertake.

Carnegie never invested in a project until its profitability had already been demonstrated. He let other people take the risks. In his early days, he only invested on inside information and leads.

Rockefeller never really went out on a limb either. He went into the oil business long after its birth, and was never quite sure if there was even enough oil bottled up inside the earth to warrant building permanent longstanding plant facilities. Rockefeller kept himself in a liquid position at all times, didn't gamble, and only expanded on what he saw to be a sure thing.

The successful businessman treads on sure ground - in the cognitive territory he is familiar with.

The successful entrepreneur bases the conduct of his affairs on business, not luck. He takes advantage of whatever capital he has; experience, knowledge, contacts, financial assets, and position.

He uses other people's money whenever possible.

He is not impulsive, but he is a plunger once he is sure. His intense acquisitive character is matched only by his tenacity. Once he makes a plan, all his energies are focused on carrying it out.

First he watches, then he plans, and finally he acts.

The producer who plans his financial future, and seriously follows that plan, will wind up on top. There are many many hamburger stands - but only one developed into the McDonald's chain. A method of selling cosmetics door-to-door was the idea seed that grew into Avon.

One simple idea, managed properly, spells success. Ask the old Kentucky Colonel who used his social security check to start a take-home fried chicken business. Or ask Hugh Hefner about Playboy.

It took twenty-five years to sell the Xerox process to a company, but that one idea catapulted a previously insignificant firm into the prominent role of becoming one of America's major companies. One idea syndicated a real estate sales program into a national organization called Red Carpet Realty.

One idea. That's all it takes. The trick is finding that creative idea, planning the steps, and putting the plan into action.

You can only make financial progress if you truly and deeply **want** to. If you are diligent, and tend your idea seed into a sapling, you may one day stand back to gaze at your accomplishments, and find a forest of towering oaks.

Chapter Seven

DESIRE, GOALS, AND PLANS

"There is all the difference in the world between treating people equally and attempting to make them equal."
Fredrich A. von Hayek

There have always been two major groups of people since the dawn of the human race - those who are moved, and those who move.

Only a few salient individuals ever stand out among the billions at any given period among the grey common impersonal mass of humanity that has lived, breathed, and died on this planet.

Those who make an impact are the ones motivated by the desire to achieve. Unless the producer **wants** to be successful, he will join the billions who have failed.

The winner must desperately **want** to succeed. He must be consumed with the burning desire to reach a definite, carefully laid out, goal. He must be obsessed with the urge to win.

The producer needs success like the common man needs air, water, food, and sleep. He needs it to survive, and will work hard, over seemingly insurmountable obstacles, at excruciating personal costs, to reach his goal.

He is motivated. Not only does he continually dream, but he is always in the acting - spelled producing - frame of mind; with the urge to succeed, and the mood to do something about it.

The producer knows there is no such thing as a free lunch. He knows that there is only one way to get something everyone recognizes is valuable - to work hard for it. He knows something for nothing is a fairy tale, and he is always aware his desire for success can only be achieved at the expense of hard work and time.

The producer implements his desire into a clearly defined goal. He wants to be top banana. He is not satisfied with being a second string player. He makes that goal a need. He puts himself in the state of mind essential to success.

Like the de-hydrated man in the desert who is weak, tired, and sun-worn, the producer who sights a water hole miles away can summon unknown inner energy and overcome painful human limitations, phsyiological costs, physical difficulty, biological obstacles, and geographic barriers to reach that goal.

He doesn't even have to think about his decision. The choice is automatic. He must achieve his goal, or else he will die.

The producer turns a dream into reality. He focuses all his energy, effort, and will power into reaching that goal. And he does everything he can to give that goal a continuous, aching mental presence.

If you want to become a producer, you must first establish, in precise terms, what your exact goal specifically is.

Get out a piece of paper.

Now write down your desires in life - money, friendship, love, sex, notoriety, peace of mind, respect, integrity, freedom, control over your own life, etc...

Think about your life's ambitions, and write down the exact amount of money you would like to have, keeping in mind your life's other objectives.

Put down what you have that you can exchange to get that money - it may be labor, real estate, imagination, stocks, bonds, an idea, cash, etc.

Write the specific date you intend to have that sum of money.

Now, outline a basic plan - the steps. Be reasonable. Include time deadlines and subgoals. Prepare to start putting that plan into action today.

Finally, write down a clear, short statement of your goal. Include how much money you are going to have, when you are going to have it, and just what you're going to do to earn it.

The firm statement of your goal will create a definiteness of purpose. A goal directs purposeful action toward a single objective. It gives the producer a reason for working. It provides a path for accomplishment, and acts as an incentive to continue; as the producer proudly looks back at what he has already been able to accomplish.

A goal is the magnet that pulls the producer along a specified course, minimizing unproductive random forays off the path.

The goal gives him a **reason** for acting, and it allows him to gauge his performance.

In order to succeed, you must convince yourself that you can do it. You must dream, wish, hope, desire, and plan.

The best way to create a success habit is to make yourself continuously aware of your goal.

One way of doing this is to read your goal twice a day -before going to bed, and just after getting up. You can say it over time and time again during the day. You could put a little note on your shaving mirror or office wall as reminders to repeat your goal.

The whole idea is to structure a pattern that puts you in frequent contact with reminders of your goal. When you are forced to remember, you put yourself into the proper frame of mind to succeed.

The producer with a conscious plan is alert to possibilities that could help propel him toward his goal. He thinks; he puts ideas together; he creates. He has the advantage over others of purposefully thinking on a third dimension.

When it comes right down to it, all riches come from ideas.

The person who is capable of creative, lateral, thought will be the one who stands the best chance of finding that unique amalgamated concept that will sell - and fetch him a fortune.

New ideas may be new inventions, new ways to do something, a new teaching method, a new service, a new combination of existing ideas, a new way to advertise, finance, or expand. The thinking producer harnesses ideas, and converts them into factories, cities, cars, airplanes, and business firms.

Ford put metal together in a new and special combination -and sold cars. Bell wrapped some wire in unusual shapes; attached it to a special series of devices and created the telephone. The producer converts ideas into money. He combines food and service to make a restaurant; a restaurant with music and drinks to make an entertainment facility; he combines the facility with shows and rides to make an amusement park; he puts together series of them into a chain; franchises the idea, rents, leases, and borrows on it. Someone else recognizes a single aspect of the operation as the focal point to create still another money-maker.

The producer bravely faces whatever fears that lie between him and his goal. He does this by changing his attitude - by refusing to settle for only half the pie; by renouncing the creed of the partial achiever.

He does it by believing in himself. This is accomplished by programming himself through the repetition of his goal (called autosuggestion). He uses the plan as the motor to reach his goal.

The producer is a practical dreamer. He thinks, and implements his ideas. He is a man of action, AND DOES NOT QUIT. He sticks fast and hard to his goal.

The producer is different from the rest of mankind. He faces an uphill effort, and has only his own self confidence to rely upon.

Everyone laughed at Columbus because he thought the

world was round. The common public jeered at the Wright brothers for trying to build a machine that would fly like a bird. Copernicus and Galileo endured physical torture for challenging the notion that the earth was at the center of the universe, and that it moved.

They all laughed at Ford, with his ideas of a "horseless carriage", at Noah and his land-locked arc; at Edison and his "light bulb."

It took Edison over 10,000 successive failures before he discovered how to make an incandescent light bulb.

Self confidence is a necessary quality to propel a man toward achieving his goal. Beethoven was deaf. Milton was blind.

Marconi's friends took him to a mental hospital after he told them how he found a way to send messages hundreds of miles through the air without a wire connection. Bell's associates thought him mad, trying to send voices through tiny little wires.

There is only one limiting roadblock to success - and that is the set of barriers we set up in our own minds.

NOTES

57

Chapter Eight

SELF CONFIDENCE

"By allowing full scope for investment, mobility, the division of labor, creativity, and entrepreneurship, the free economy thereby creates the conditions for rapid economic development."

Murray Rothbard

It is no easy process to physically transmute desire into money. You must first convince your subconscious mind that everything must be done to achieve your goal.

Any idea or plan can be engraved inside your mind through repetition. Once that plan is etched in the subconscious, purposeful activity toward a goal becomes automatic.

The producer should write down his principal aim, and keep repeating it until memorized and firmly imprinted inside the subconscious mind.

The vibrations of purposeful thought will permeate the dormant uninspired corners of your mind, resonating all thought patterns. They will harmonize your pursuits and activities along a reasoned, planned, constructive, progressive plan of action.

Once dominated by your goal, it becomes all-enveloping. You are motivated to reach that goal. You become uneasy, because there is an urge inside you crying to be filled. As a result, you are **driven** toward a definitive objective, along the avenues of your plans.

The person without a plan, and who is without self confidence, will lead a life of purposeless random misdirected bursts of energy. Together, his achievements will add up to zero.

If only he had **directed** those bursts of energy toward a

58

result, he would have accomplished something.

The producer can detect progress, as he sticks to and moves along his plan. He is able to watch the approaching goal get closer and closer. He can practically visualize grasping his objective. He builds self confidence.

As Napoleon Hill states, "Assuredness is the only known antidote for failure."

The self confident producer has faith in both himself as well as his goal. And faith transforms a thought of common importance into one with spiritual significance.

Once you **know** you can reach your goal, you will.

The acquisition of self confidence is built after envy, jealousy, and hate, have been thrown away. The producer realizes that he will create wealth if he makes money, and the only way to make money is by providing something that benefits all the people involved in any nonforceful voluntary transaction. He will benefit if others benefit. He will make money by providing a service; by meeting a need.

The producer respects humanity. He worships man qua man, and looks upon people as the only real source of wealth.

Repetition of his goal develops a purpose to life, and laminates his desire into persistence for attaining his goal.

He autosuggestively converts thoughts into action by inculcating perseverence into his thought processes. And perseverence is the key to success. Perseverence makes the producer stay in there when things appear hopeless; perseverence pulls him off the floor when he is down; perseverence fills his mind with the spiritual drive to keep moving ahead.

The producer should repeat his goals aloud; imagining that he can see and feel the actual goal in his hands.

Repeat your goals in a quiet, private place. Tell yourself how badly (and how much) you want to accumulate. Remind yourself of your time frame. Remember what you're offering in return for wealth, and motivate yourself to provide the **best** service you can.

You will perform to the best of your capabilities. Direct your voluntary conscious mind. Use it as a tool to reach inside and influence the subconscious mind.

It was only a couple decades ago that a milkshake mixer salesman turned one San Bernardino hamburger stand into a vast fast foods empire. That was Ray Kroc, and the company he built is McDonald's.

Ray Kroc has a few words to say about the value of perseverence:

Press On!

Nothing in the world can take the
place of perseverence.
Talent will not; nothing is
more common than unsuccessful
men with talent.
Genius will not; unrewarded
genius is almost a proverb.
Education alone will not;
the world is full of educated derelicts.
Persistence and determination
alone are omnipotent.

It is a fact that more people have given up the game at the goal line simply because they didn't know they were there, than at any other point on the field. Just one more try, one more bit of stubborn determination could have carried them on to success.

Why didn't they know? First, because they didn't fully understand what they were doing, and second, they lacked the confidence that knowledge would have given them. It takes all three to make a dream into reality.

The person who perseveres is destined to succeed. Talent, genius, education, and even money are worthless without it. Only personal dedication to a goal by a self-assured person will do it. When the going gets tough, the tough get going sums it up.

If this sounds like a lot simplified hogwash or a Sunday school sermon, you are missing the point. The most difficult things to accomplish are most often the most simple to comprehend. Becoming successful in the field you have chosen is simple to understand, but not simple to do. And only by really meaning to do it, will you do it.

This then is the beginning - the place to take the first step on your journey to a goal. Let's recap the procedure.

NOTES

Chapter Nine

KNOW WHAT YOU ARE DOING

"Were we directed from Washington when to sow, and when to reap, we should soon want bread."

Thomas Jefferson

General knowledge is the stuff that's taught inside universities. It consists of general, universal theories; principals and extensions; incontestable facts needed for a "well-rounded" education.

Every major university has a string of economics professors, men and women who are long on theory and advice; short on money.

General knowledge is very important, and it certainly helps to have some. But general knowledge is not what the producer needs a lot of if he wants to make money.

Specific knowledge is worth money; knowing where a **specific** thing is at a particular time; how it can be used; for how long; and what for.

There was once a contractor digging up streets in an old neighborhood. His crews kept hitting gas mains, so he sent away for an expert who promised to locate the pipes before the machinery even started digging.

A polished graduate from one of America's finer universities showed up on the construction sight, with an electronic gadget that was supposed to detect underground pipes. He passed over the road until the needle on his machine deflected, and the crews were directed where to dig. In no time at all, they were striking gas mains again.

The contractor sent away for a good 'ol Southern boy, who claimed he could accurately locate the pipes without any automatic devices.

The Southerner bent a welding iron into the shape of a divining rod, and walked down the center of the road outlining the actual exact pathway of the underground gas pipe.

Only useful, organized knowledge attracts money.

If the producer has a definite end in mind (his goal), a plan of action, and is subconsciously motivated to activate his plan as a result of autosuggestion, he may creatively arrange his specialized knowledge into an idea that can be converted into money.

Education (General knowledge) comes from formal institutional instruction. Specialized knowledge is learned, not taught.

All occupations demand specialists, and any opportunity to make money requires specialized knowledge.

Once the producer knows his goal, he has already narrowed down the field of specialized knowledge he should know.

Andrew Carnegie knew nothing about the technical process of making steel. His knowledge was organizational, and probably would have been just as useful in any other industry. He directed the firm, was a skillful manager, and knew how to allocate authority. Carnegie assigned the other areas of specialized knowledge to others.

The producer must know what he is doing. He can be totally ignorant of general knowledge, but he **must** be an expert in the field, and have adequate specialized knowledge.

Many people try going into business without having the faintest idea or understanding of the specialized knowledge necessary to make the venture a success. Blind enthusiasm, and nothing else, ensures failure. The desire to succeed, just by itself, is important, but it is not enough.

The thinking person wouldn't sit down to a card game, and bet heavily, if he didn't know the rules. But that's precisely what many people do who go into business themselves for the first time.

Many people stake their life's savings and future hopes on a game they don't even know the rules to. They don't know how many cards they will get, they can't see the cards once they are dealt, and they don't know what or how to bet.

Such a strategy is doomed to failure.

The producer should be knowledgeable of the activity he has undertaken.

NOTES

Chapter Ten

ORGANIZED PLANNING

"In a free economy, in which wages, costs, and prices are left to the free play of the competitive market, the prospect of profits decides what articles will be made, and in what quantities - and what articles will not be made at all."

Henry Hazlitt

The producer must set a goal, develop a plan, and single-mindedly dedicate his efforts toward reaching that goal. He must respect his fellow man as an individual entitled with human integrity. He must recognize the significance of the mutually beneficial process of voluntary exchange and at the same time remain emotionally detached in his dealings with people.

The producer derives immense enjoyment from seeing himself get closer to his goal. He does not take defeat on the chin. He has definite plans and decisions. He has self control, courage to act, and a habit of doing more than is expected of him, or more than he is paid for. He has a pleasing personality, a sense of fairness, sympathy, and understanding. The producer has a cooperative character, a willingness to take responsibility, and a detailed understanding of the specialized knowledge that helps him solve problems that must be hurdled on the way toward achieving his goal.

The producer is able to organize details, is willing to perform humble services, has no fear of underlings, is imaginative, does not seek to acquire credit that belongs to others, and de-emphasizes the "authority" behind leadership.

He provides quality service, is agreeable, and brims with the spirit of harmonious conduct.

The producer converts his ideas into money by combining specialized knowledge with imagination through the active implementation of organized plans.

He has a creative imagination. He thinks differently from others — in another dimension. He uses lateral thought processes to interpret things differently than other people. He goes on hunches and moments of inspiration. He sharpens his creative imagination through its constant use.

The producer **knows** he will succeed, and is obsessed by the desire to achieve. One good idea, coupled with an organized plan, will jettison anyone into fiscal stardom.

The organized planner keeps his goal in sight, and channels everything he has toward reaching that goal. He puts himself into a frame of mind that converts the voluntary plan into reflexive instincts.

Repetition autosuggestively makes his plan a habit. His automatic reactions are cultivated, and he is enabled to efficiently achieve his goals. He uses the thought processes of the conscious mind to alter the brain patterns of the subconscious.

The non-producer worries over fear. The producer transmutes fear into productive energy. He is a problem solver, an achiever, a barrier dissolver. Fear of poverty, fear of bad health, or fear of insecure finances is converted into action that relieves the productive efforts.

Many producers sublimate the sex drive into productive efforts. They harness and transmute the sexual drive along channels that help activate the producer toward reaching his goal.

Sex transmutation gears up the producer's thoughts to a high pitch. And when the mind has already been stimulated, the creative mind starts to function.

It is no accident that creative thought operates during conversations, debates, writing, music, fear, love, friendship, or sex - at times the mind is already at an active level.

The organized planner is constantly aware of his goal - and the plan he is using to reach it. He is always thinking and coming up with new ideas. All he has to do is concentrate on the completed part of his plan - looking at both the near and ultimate objectives - he will always be engaged in constructive activity leading in the direction of his goal.

Many of the people who accumulated vast fortunes did so because they **had** to. They were **driven** by the **need** to succeed.

Persistence is the banner of the organized planner. Persistence is the state of mind cultivated by a clear cut goal, a plan to reach that goal, and progress that can be seen, measured, and gauged over time.

The organized planner looks upon himself as the physical manufacturing plant of a fortune. He has definite plans, - the ability to follow through with plans - a burning desire, self-reliance, accurate knowledge, reflexive goal-oriented habits, a cooperative mentality, and an obsession to concentrate thought on both the goal and the means necessary to reach that goal.

The organized planner is not impressed by short-cut-to-riches schemes.

He develops persistence by backing purpose with the urge for fulfillment. He has a plan in continuous motion. His mind is closed to any and all disturbing influences.

NOTES

Chapter Eleven

BLUEPRINT TO RICHES

"Rights are conditions of existence required by man's nature for his proper survival. If man is to live on earth, it is right for him to use his mind, it is right to act on his own free judgment, it is right to work for his values and to keep the product of his work. If life on earth is his purpose, he has the right to live as a rational being. Nature forbids him the irrational."

Ayn Rand

The nuts and bolts behind every fortune are more than just simple motivation. Riches come when desire is coupled with a goal, plan, and lots of hard work.

Financial success is achieved through a four-part formula. First you must plan, then save, finally invest, and always compound.

No one can succeed without a plan. You have to know where you are going if you are going to have a chance at all of getting there. The producer must be motivated to implement that plan. He becomes successful when he reaches his goal, or passes by each subgoal within the budgeted time frame.

Once the producer knows where he is going, and has made the commitment to get there, he must take the first step—by squirrelling away money in a savings plan.

One of the best ways to painlessly save is by taking 10% out of every pay check before you even start spending your money. Pay your bills and meet your expenses. Spend as little as you have to. Then save some more.

The beginning stages are the most important. The sooner you invest and get your money working for you, the sooner your money is pumped into interest spiral, and the longer it

71

has a chance to earn interest on top of interest. Pennies that are saved today may be thousands of dollars in the years to come.

John D. Rockefeller only earned $13.46 a week as a wholesale clerk. He didn't smoke, drink, or play pool. And he saved $1,000 in just two and a half years -enough money for the 19 year old to go into a commission business partnership.

Cornelius Vanderbilt saved $1,000 by the time he was 18, and had $9,000 when he was 23.

You can save even on a small salary. And you have to save before you invest. The example of the seven day laborer brothers in the second chapter illustrates the meaning of savings hooked into a steady investment program.

The sooner you can get your money earning interest, the longer it will compound the interest over and over again. As the many examples in chapters 1 and 2 show, a little pool of savings left to compound and grow over time can become a giant lake or ocean.

Had you invested $1 at the start of the American Revolution, and left the growing sum untouched, your family would have $466,000 by the year 2000 - had it been allowed to compound at 6%. Had it grown at 10% rate, your family would have almost two **billion** dollars. Had one dollar been multiplied just by 15% each year it would have grown to 260 times as much as today's Gross National Product!

With a plan you can speed this process up. The more you save today, the more you can invest - and the faster your assets will grow.

NOTES

73

Chapter Twelve

MAKING IT IN HARD TIMES

*"With some, the word liberty may mean for each man to
do as he pleases with himself, and the product of his labor;
while with others, the same word may mean for some men to
do as they please with other men, and the product of other
man's labor."*

Abraham Lincoln

It doesn't take a genius to make money when times are
good. But how are you going to maintain your financial
growth rate during an economic slump?

Believe it or not, there **are** some ways to strike it rich in
hard times.

Joe Kennedy, the patriarch of the famous Kennedy clan,
found his big break at the start of the great depression. When
the bottom fell out of the market and everybody else was
madly selling their stocks at discounted prices, Joe Kennedy
was buying up everything in sight.

There is profit to be made in every set of economic conditions.

Let's take a look at the four basic stages of the business cycle
as it is turning near the peak, and see how the producer can
profit in **either** boom **or** bust.

First, we have to know how to recognize the cycles.

During the first stage, savings deposits are up, purchases of
capital equipment are down, new car sales even off or ease
downward.

People are very optimistic. They exaggerate earnings expectations of companies, and bid stock prices up to high
price/earnings ratios. A correcting mechanism goes into motion. Stock prices are discounted to reasonable levels with the

pressure that is exerted on interest rates.

Interest rates are maintained at low levels by government authorities (who are no doubt trying to encourage capital equipment purchases). Interest rates **want** to rise, but they are restrained at an artificially low level from doing so.

Interest rates rise slightly during the second stage. People lower their expectations of corporate earnings, and stock prices fall. Inventories drop. Plant construction tapers off, the demand for luxury items such as furs and boats falls. The institutional investors pull out of long term investment. They put their money into "blue chips" and short term investments.

Retail sales are down in the third stage. Steel production drops, and we start hearing about lay-offs in the auto industry. Interest rates settle down, losing their urge to rise. The unemployment rate rises.

Unemployment rates explode in the fourth stage, new home construction takes a dive, retail sales are down, reports of bankruptcies and business failures make the news, interest rates are low, and nobody wants to borrow money.

One of the ways to make money in hard times is to put your assets in some of the businesses that traditionally do well **because** there is a recession.

Since times are hard, and people buy fewer durable goods, the repair business prospers. Whether the business repairs TVs, appliances, air conditioners, radios, shoes, sewing machines, tires, or typewriters, its sales volume will rise.

For the same reason, auto part stores, discount stores, do-it-yourself items, thrift shops, used cars, and used equipment experience a growing market during recessions.

The demand for cheaper entertainment stimulates sales in books, camping equipment, birth control devices, fishing equipment, sporting goods, smoking supplies, and utilities (people stay home more).

Drug stores, hardware stores, paint stores, laundermats, mail order houses, leasing services, and rental services all do well in a recession.

Printing, publishing, paper, postage services (more mail is sent during recessions) are all good businesses to get into during hard times.

Financial advisory services likewise encounter an expanding market of worried investors.

The things to stay clear of in a recession are furs, jewelry, flowers, luggage, new aircraft, cars, and office equipment, boats, luxury entertainment, live theatre, travel agencies, and musical instruments.

NOTES

Chapter Thirteen

THE PRODUCER'S PHILOSOPHY

"The future of private enterprise capitalism is also the future of a free society. There is no possibility of having a politically free society unless the major part of its economic resources are operated under a capitalistic private enterprise system."

Milton Friedman

Throughout history, man has been dominated, regulated, directed, registered, stamped, numbered, authorized, licensed, commanded, checked, inspected, watched, and law-ridden by government.

Of all people, the producer has been the one who has been the most castigated, admonished, spat upon, ridiculed, restricted, moralized, censured, and taxed.

History is a soap opera of destroyed civilizations.

Time and time again, civilized societies have crumbled into barbarism. Mandatory edict overruled voluntary individual choice, force supplanted cooperation, exchange was replaced by seizure, the individual became a dispensable unit of the collective, muscle ruled mind. and dialogues became directions.

Societies are destroyed whenever individual integrity fails to be respected. Whenever individual rights have been crushed by government, the destruction of human liberty has been followed by economic chaos and continued political degeneration.

Like the moth attracted to a brightly lit lantern, there seems to be an almost instinctual urge inside politicians to keep returning to the flame of collectivism - even though their wings keep getting singed.

Why has society forsaken the individual? Why are we so attracted to collectivist solutions to government-created problems?

Television broadcasters report the earnings of corporations as if they were describing an ax murder. They use words like "all-time-high", "record", or "windfall" profits like they would use the word "sodomy."

Every productive American faces a steeply graduated and deeply punitive income tax. The clear message from Washington is "Don't make money. Don't produce."

In what has come to be an annual ritual, the IRS goes on stage shortly after income taxes are due, to announce the number of wealthy individuals who had been lucky enough to costlessly and legally slip through the loopholes in the IRS drag net.

Is the producer supposed to do penance for the "sin" of profit? Is he supposed to apologize for being successful, and making money?

You'd better get ready to come in contact with the dominant ideology of the non-producer. At least 75% of the people you come in contact with would like to tax you, criticize you, assault you, and envy you because you are or want to be, a success.

If you are not sustained by the indelible urge to succeed, you are playing a game with odds heavily stacked against you. Nobody is on the side of the producer these days. The parasites in government will burden every move you make. Then they will penalize you with higher and higher taxes in the event you are successful - in spite of their interference.

The only way you are going to make it is by relying on nobody but yourself. The purpose of this final chapter is to add a spiritual dimension to the pursuit of wealth. Call profit anything you like, but please don't call it dirty.

Profit is the mainspring of human progress.

Business has been defined as mutual benefit. Every business transaction is a voluntary exchange of valuable items between a buyer and seller.

The free market is characterized by voluntary exchange taking place among free men. No exchange takes place unless it is mutually beneficial to all parties concerned. Voluntary exchange makes society better off as a whole. Free trade is the keystone for social cooperation, peaceful interhuman relations, and economic progress.

An individual makes money in a competitive market by serving the consuming public with a product or service they desire. He can only make money if he fills the most urgent wants of the consumers. The better he serves the public, the more he can sell. And the more he sells, the richer he becomes.

Those producers who best serve the consumers make the most profits, and may expand their businesses. Those who do a poor job lose money, and must restrict their scale of operation. Competitive private enterprise guarantees that profits direct the production of all goods. Through profits, producers make decisions about what to do. Resources are directed to meet the demands most intensely felt by the consumer.

The free market price system is responsible for keeping a centralized mechanism with consumers democratically deciding for themselves what they want, how much they want, and how much they are willing to pay.

Individual producers scurrying around to satisfy those wants are patronized only if they provide what is demanded.

The system of government stands in striking contrast to the market place. Government decisions are formulated by people who think themselves morally superior to the people they regulate.

Authoritarian government agencies issue edicts that must be obeyed. There is no matter of choice on the part of the consumer **or** producer.

The free market is responsible for the freedom enjoyed by the world's western democracies. Free trade necessitates the use of private property, which carries with it the **right** to act, not contingent on any grant or license from any governmental unit.

Private property forms the supporting pillar for both economic and civil liberty. It gives man the individual right to act. We would not have freedom of the press if the government could tell the press what it could and could not print. And if government owned the printing presses, they would exercise control over printing.

Only because printing presses are privately owned do we have freedom of the press.

In a like manner, we wouldn't have freedom in religion if the government owned the places of worship, or outlined how religious facilities could be used. Nor would there continue to be freedom of speech if the government owned all the areas of assembly.

Private property and the free market form the basis of civilized society. As a producer striving after profits in the market place, you should be proud of the role you play for American liberty.

Don't be discouraged when the current mass ideology clouds the horizon. Remember your role. Be proud of it. Don't be afraid to correct those people who pervert the name of profit.

NOTES

THE BIOGRAPHY OF MILLIONAIRES

Most people think that millionaires are very special people who are unique in their talents and gifts for making money.

But this simply is not true. In fact, oftentimes millionaires start out as plain everyday working people just like you or me and they "discover" the secrets that will be revealed to you — once you've read all seven magical money manuals —

And once you've discovered the secrets — and learn how to effectively put them into action, success — "Super Success" can easily become yours.

This special report is about what it takes to become a millionaire — A self-made millionaire today — **This Year** ... It's a critical study of the backgrounds, character traits, drives and motivation that I genuinely believe are required to become extremely successful — And Very Very Rich.

This biographical sketch of what it takes to become a self-made millionaire is based on a composite study I performed on more than 35 self-made millionaires I have personally known and observed.

I encourage anyone who craves the unexcelled independence that true financial freedom can bring to thoroughly study this revealing report and strive to incorporate as many of these **"Success-Proven"** traits as possible into your own millionaire's strategy.

First — In order to ever hope to become a millionaire you must believe it **is** possible.

In my own personal studies of self-made millionaires, I've observed the fact that each and every one of them believed — beyond a shadow of a doubt — that he or she **would** become successful. Believed too that he or she deserved to attain super success. In order to become super successful, you **must** first be able to not only believe in yourself ... **but** you also must be able to visualize yourself becoming the success you

84

desire.

Until you can see yourself acting, being and attaining the role of a millionaire — you haven't a chance of achieving this lofty goal. Yet once you break down the "visualization barrier" that most men and women erect in their minds — once you can honestly visualize yourself becoming (and deserving) Super Successful — the rest is literally downhill.

To get from point A to point B you must first have a plan

. . .

Of the 35 self-made millionaires I have studied the closest — all but one of them achieved super success swiftly because they had created a master plan of success (and of Pro-gress) long ago — and they possessed solid stair stepping techniques to securely propel them from one success level — up to another — and on to another until they ultimately catapulted themselves all the way to the top.

And an essential part of literally every millionaire's success-plan was to think in terms of **finite** goals and objectives — plus a timetable to schedule themselves strictly in order to meet their short term objectives.

One character trait I personally feel is paramount in enabling you to adhere to a Finite-oriented success plan is a keen degree of self discipline. If you currently are not good at visualizing your goals — if you have great difficulty in initiating positive action on your own — without any assistance — I strongly urge you to know — at the very beginning of your quest for super success — that you must develop and cultivate a strong sense of self-reliance and resourcefulness.

If you are not used to being self-reliant or you're not experienced at visualizing objectives in finite terms — here are some tricks you might try.

First — After thoroughly studying all seven of my money manuals — I recommend that you try to "zero" in on the combination of money making techniques that are best suited

85

for you. Once you've selected the very best series of money making variables — try to put them together to form a workable success concept. Experiment until the combination of money making techniques comes together into a strategy you personally feel comfortable with.

Then — Once you've developed your own workable technique — try to visualize the easiest way to quickly put it into profitable action — not trying to make a million dollars the first time out.

Then — calculate what you need to do — starting today — immediately to put this plan into action — and determine what you **must** do each and every day in order to keep your newly created "money-machine" operating and building up "profit-momentum" as I like to call it.

As you start vividly seeing your money machine materialize before your very eyes, write down your conclusions on a pad of paper. Once you've completely detailed your objective, break down your NEW goal by stairsteps. In other words — in order to own and control the profitable money machine you are finally visualizing you must first accomplish a number of things. Identify each necessary step in accomplishing your success-goal, then prioritize them in order of progression. Your "money-machine" goal might be to build a company that owns 100 rental homes. And if today when you first visualize this goal you have no such company — and own no such rental homes — you obviously must perform all of the following steps: Form a company. Develop a source of financing. Select areas you want to operate in. Start looking at homes for sale. Start researching the income property markets, etc.

In my interviews with super-successful self-made millionaires I've learned a trick for turning seemingly overwhelming objectives into easily Accomplished Goals —

All you have to do is learn how to disect an objective into

its sum total parts — then identify the prioritized manner in which each part comes together to build the successful organization — and attack the first part first — the second part second — and so on until finally — often before you even know it — you've easily and successfully accomplished your total goal — and you're well on your way to success and wealth you've always dreamed of achieving.

And it's remarkably easy to do really. Here's all it takes:

If you're going to start out part-time on your newly selected wealth-path, allocate to yourself no less than one hour a day (and preferably two or more) that you will dutifully spend pursuing your goal on a strictly prioritized manner.

Then start doing just that. And whatever you do, don't jump around from step one to step three or step three to step seven.

In all my studies of great successes, the one most consistent observation I made about these men and women was that they all followed a strict formula of doing everything on a simple progressive step-by-step basis — and they made absolutely sure that every step was done right — and done as completely as possible — before they would ever think of moving on to the next step. And by doing this, they were confident in the knowledge that the money-machine they were building was built right — was solid — would not break down — and would definitely last.

Unless you strictly follow these same principles, you cannot possibly expect to build any type of a money machine that will last **or** flourish. And if you do endeavor to circumvent this irrefutable set of long term wealth principles, any short term successes you might achieve will certainly be **very** short lived.

The next ingredient I discovered in virtually every super-success I studied was the keen ability to leverage oneself many times over. In order to fully comprehend the real significance that self-leveraging holds to super success, I must illustrate various examples of this powerful money-making technique in action.

If you determine that you want to pursue a specific course of wealth building, you have two courses of action you could potentially pursue. The first — and certainly the easiest to get started — is to do it all yourself — a one-man show without a big organization ... and this is actually the very best way to start out. **But** it is also the most difficult technique through which to become super successful.

The reason is quite simple.

As a one man show you are severely restricted in the amount of effort you can possibly exert towards accomplishment of your goals. For example — if you decided to deal in rental homes, you only have a finite number of hours you can possibly dedicate to this business of your own by yourself every day. It may be 8 hours or it may be 14 hours. Nevertheless, you still have a restrictive ceiling placed upon you as to the number of prospective homes you are capable of viewing in a day, week, month — or the number of units you are capable of buying, managing, maintaining, etc. ...

But, suddenly through the near magic of leveraging yourself, you can amazingly duplicate your efforts many times over and the results can be equally astounding.

Plus — there are any number of different leveraging techniques you can employ — each one of which can increase your results remarkably — and the incorporation of all of them creates a geometric profit progression the likes of which most beginning wealth builders cannot begin to comprehend.

FOR EXAMPLE —

If as a one man show you could only afford to look at three prospective homes a day (21 a week) ... and you average making an offer on 20% of the homes you looked at — and

normally ended up buying 10% of the ones you bid on —
you'd be actually only buying one house a month.

What would happen if you recruited another person to
assist you — a person who knew exactly what criteria you
were looking for in the prospective rental homes you sought
to buy. What if you could have your "assistant" spend **full
time** — 8 hours a day — looking at prospective properties,
and selecting only the most deserving ones for you to actually
come in and bid on?

If you acquired such an assistant, he or she could probably
look at up to 20 homes a day, 140 a week, and if the same
percentage figure held up, you could end up buying up to
seven homes a month, assuming you could handle the financing.

And that's only leveraging yourself 100%.

What if you hired two full time assistants to look at homes
for you — three full time assistants — five — ten — or
more???

You can quickly see how you could duplicate your efforts
many many times over.

But that's just on one side of the business.

What about managing the homes once you buy them.

Sure, when you start you can easily handle it yourself, but
as your "holdings" start increasing, what happens if you
"leverage" yourself on the management side as well — by
hiring a full or part time asistant to handle the management
end — allowing you to devote full time to bidding on the
"desirable" properties your assistants locate for you.

And that's still just the tip of the leveraging "Iceberg."
You can leverage yourself "financially" by taking in financial partners to put up the necessary funding to allow you to
buy more homes.

You can leverage yourself occupancy wise by hiring either a
full time rental agency or by making commission referral

deals with all the realtors around your area.

The possibilities are nearly unlimited.

But first, remember the basics — establish a solid, well built structure and expand out progressively, paying great attention to broadening your support base as your income increases.

You can adapt the miracle profit powers of leveraging to virtually any viable endeavor with equally exciting results.

In Selling, for example, one man — you can only humanly make so many calls a day — but if you had five other salesmen working for you, ten, twenty or more, each one making you money — you could quickly earn twenty times as much as you could possibly make doing it all yourself.

And leveraging is only limited by your own creative applications — the sky literally is the limit — as long as you build **always** on a base that is solid enough to support your growth.

Another particularly important trait that I discovered most self-made millionaires possessed was what I call empirical foresight. You might better know it as having a contingency plan.

Put simply, the truly successful people I know and studied realize going into a new venture that everything doesn't always go according to plan. Oftentimes things go quite differently, in fact. So the shrewd business men and women take the time in advance of making fatal mistakes to predetermine **every** possible result — good or bad — that can conceivably occur and they **develop** contingency **or** "back up" plans that they can quickly initiate and put into action in the event that a given plan doesn't go as smoothly as expected.

And quite remarkably, I've discovered that there normally are only a "finite" number of ways any and every situation can possibly go — and anyone willing to spend a few hours of objective thinking prior to embarking on a new business venture can easily identify the finite number of possibilities to ever expect to happen to them.

And once identified in advance, even the worst possible occurence or reversal can be calmly prepared for well in advance of its occurence, and a workable alternative plan of action can be ready and waiting to be implemented if ever the need arises.

More "seat-of-the-pants" entrepreneurs get their jeans caught in this trap than any other.

They tend to be so overwhelmingly optimistic that they fail to ever concede the possibility that their venture won't go exactly according to plan — and when it doesn't, they get caught completely off guard and are not capable of counter programming quickly enough to save the venture.

You would actually be surprised at just how many millionaires started out with ventures that **did not** go according to their optimistic plans and were it not for brilliant strategic "contingency" planning these shrewd entrepreneurs had done in advance, many would never have become successful at all!!

Which brings me to another very significant attribute that every self-made millionaire I studied possessed — Resiliency. Without breaking your illusions, the reality of money-making is that in order to succeed really greatly, you oftentimes must fail miserably — and sometimes fail more than once. The truly great self-made successes I studied demonstrated an ultra durable disposition and a very special type of resiliency that allowed them to bounce right back from whatever short-term failures they might have encountered — and literally pick themselves up, dust themselves off and jump right back into the ring of competition, ready to fight for success smarter than ever, profiting greatly by remembering the costly mistakes they had made earlier in their business careers.

You, too, should mentally prepare yourself for the

possibility of failure along the road to super success. Some degree of failure is almost certain to occur — if only to bring you back to the realization that you, too, are only mortal and do in fact make mistakes.

Expect your failures or setbacks to occur for one of the following reasons, for these are the most prominent:
• Over optimism
• Failure to properly gauge the real success quotient
• Failure to prepare contingency plans
• Business inexperience
• Lack of sufficient capital
• Rapid expansion without building a solid base of support
• Failure to analyze market
• Failure to properly leverage

One of the inside secrets you'll learn if you every study self-made millionaires is their ability to avoid setbacks by securing very capable mentors.

Unlike the old adage that states "you only learn from your mistakes" — the self-made millionaire endeavors to associate with a highly experienced business person, or group of persons, who dispense invaluable advice based upon their own past business experiences.

By listening and conceding these "mentors" competence, the smart entrepreneur can learn priceless lessons before he or she has to make costly mistakes.

Finding a mentor or group of mentors (oftentimes referred to as a "master mind" group) is easier than you might expect.

In any field you might consider pursuing, you can always find some successful leader who is willing to share with you insights in his business — particularly if you pose no immediate threat or if you approach him or her in a scholastic type manner that is flattering to his ego.

Likewise, you can amass a powerful group of allies by approaching various people who can profit from your own successes and offering them participatory involvement in various aspects of your venture in exchange for not just their respective services, but their on-going advice and counsel as well.

It is fascinating to observe how much incisive advice people will tender if they, too, expect to profit from your success. Try it yourself — you'll truly be amazed.

Perseverence — tenacity — stick-to-it-iveness — call it whatever you like. The super successful people I studied all had it — and still have it. They knew that if something good was easy to do, the whole world would probably be doing it; consequently, they realized early in their pursuit of super success that you must really presevere — and if you start off really slow, stick with it. The motto I best remember is:

Make a bit of forward progress each and every day. Do not be satisfied with yourself unless you do progress every day further upward towards your defined goal.

It matters not how great or small your daily progression might be — for it all has the cumulative effect after awhile of one gigantic staircase comprised of hundreds of small, easy steps which individually amount to very little, yet together are capable of carrying you to incredible heights.

If super success is your objective, be prepared from the onset to persevere **until** you have finally attained your goal — or a more realistic goal you have chosen.

And be prepared to constantly learn — by reading, by asking, by osmosis and by listening.

Don't be afraid to study the lives of self-made people like I did — or study the lives of successful people in the field of endeavor you have selected. Biographies on numerous self-made people can be acquired from any decent library — and I doubt that any successful businessman or woman would refuse an interview with you if you told them you admired them and wanted to pattern your own business career after theirs.

Don't be afraid, also, to study other aspects of business — aspects that can help you better mold yourself into a well-rounded business person.

My own preference in self-help literature include reference material on accounting, marketing, advertising, promotion, public relations, strategy building exercises (i.e. chess, tennis) direct-selling books, direct marketing publications and countless periodicals.

I recommend that you at least sample these fine publications:

Books
Think and Grow Rich
Biography of James Ling
The Success System That Never Fails
Psycho Cybernetics

Magazines
Free Enterprise
International Entrepreneurs
Success Unlimited
Money

I also encourage you to try and personally meet and spend time interviewing some self-made, successful people. Ask them to recount for you their entire success stories. Ask them to reveal to you their current formula for success. Ask them for some solid advice. Ask them, too, to reveal the pitfalls to avoid.

And listen to what they have to say. Not only will it be revealing, it will be inspiring — and motivating as well. Then, after you've done that, go back to all seven success manuals and re-read each one carefully with particular care to glean every bit of pertinent information that can help make your personal pursuit of success even easier to achieve.

PRINCIPLES OF SUCCESS

The following biographies are presented to the reader for a number of reasons. Certainly the lives of others who have achieved their goals can be an inspiration to any of us, wealthy or not. Our lives are ours to do with as we please and it should be obvious to anyone that a successful person is one to whom we should all look as a source of knowledge. Training itself can only be fruitful when the teacher is accomplished in his field.

This points up to one of the secrets of those about whom we have been reading. They were all eager students. Not in the traditional school sense, but more in the realm of what they needed to know to accomplish their goals. They learned quickly that where they acquired their knowledge was unimportant. The value was in knowing.

They were all followers in knowledge before becoming leaders. As a German author stated, "Success is the direct effect of preparation for success." No one can achieve success without being prepared. This does not mean that one should acquire the knowledge of the world. What it does mean is that each of us should be prepared to learn the things necessary to achieve our goals.

Be it art, science or business, any accomplishment is first of all measured in competence. In fact, competence and success are equivalent. One is the measure of capacity, the other its experienced condition.

Success, of course, is always measured in some kind of achievement. The vocation chosen is not our primary concern here because it is always a product of psychological factors. The issue we have chosen to deal with in our analysis is the acquisition of wealth.

But what we want to know is how to measure achievement. Why does money flow more to some than others? By what standard can we gauge the flow.

It is the standard of being the best! To be alive is best. To know that life offers the best is to think the best. And to think the best thoughts is to live so. And how are we to do this? By always doing more and doing it better. What more could life ask of us? We live in a universe of livingness and to always be trying to make life better is a virtue in itself. Think the best thoughts and be the best.

A proper attitude toward life itself is the foundation of all positive thought. Life itself is a positive principle. And that includes all people living it. The benevolence of nature has provided us all with our existence. We come into the world with a host of assets all designed for the purpose of successful living. There are no options to life. The only option we have is the choice of living to the maximum of our capabilities or wasting away our precious lives. Life gives to us whatever we give to it. It is that simple.

Service is the cornerstone of all successful social life and the multiplier in all business success. The assets presented on financial statements are the monetary representation of the combined efforts of any number of people involved in a business. What we call capital in the form of cash, accounts receivable, machinery and other physical assets are only a small part of the whole. The people behind a business venture are the ones who either make it or break it. Of course, the most important asset in any business would be the customers. Without them, there is no business.

To get right to the heart of the matter, we cannot stress too much this all important factor of service. Everything else done in business is centered around this one activity. Progress is highly important, and it is the progress of one's customers that should be the focal point. Every added value to the clientele one serves is a prerequisite to one's own financial gain.

All competition is competition for customers. Service is, and always has been, the means of eliminating competition. This does not necessarily mean a personal service as such. Service can appear in many ways; lower prices, better products, time savers, comfort, intellectual food, better health, and hosts of other factors. The element of success in each case is that extra added value that is of benefit to the customer.

All of us are consumers and all of us are shoppers. It is that little extra here and there that we look for when we do our shopping. And it will always be the business that provides it that we will buy from.

Being the best at one's vocation is always an assurance of rising to the top. Of course the rise will not be immediate as there are many pitfalls and temporary obstacles along the way. One will have to deal with envy, jealousy, greed, dishonesty, and other negative aspects in the character of people. But these will always be temporary considerations to the person who has goals to reach. The goal and reaching it are the main focus of the successful person.

Human history evidences that the course of humanity is toward higher and higher integration. From villages, to city-states, to nation-states has taken thousands of years. It is the march of people onward and upward. No one knows as yet when it will be that we will form a global community. That in itself must of necessity be the goal of all of us. To continue under the present state of political affairs can only mean world disaster. Before we colonize the solar system, of which our planet is a part, we are all going to have to make serious and profound changes within ourselves. Those who do so will be successful within themselves regardless of how much money they have.

You are the prime mover in your life and it is your thought that you move first. You are where you are because your thought has brought you there. Blaming the world or anyone else is to no avail. Your thought creates the mind of your life and if you do not like your present station, you can change it by changing your thinking. We all have to sooner or later anyway. It is in the nature of all progress that we do so.

Since we live in a human community, finding the people who are most competent in their vocations is an ability that all successful people acquire. Napoleon Hill titled it "The Master Mind Principle" and anyone who desires achievement in life would do well to study his work. No one can make it alone. Moreover, the cardinal principle in choosing associates is to look for those who share our goals. A diversity of goals among one's associates means a diversity of effort and a dissipation of energy. Achievement is the direct opposite of dissipation.

High level goals demand high level thinking and constant striving. Our goals are represented in our values and it is our thought world that creates those values. To achieve any goal has within it all of the intermediate steps in getting there. The more clear we are, the more definitely we are able to outline the steps, the easier it becomes. And here is the point. Our capacity for any achievement in life is always a product of what we think we can do. How far we can go is always a product of available knowledge. Assuming the things we need to know are available, the remainder is simply a matter of choice. Thinking big or thinking small is of our own choosing. We will only go as far as our thought carries us.

To change one's thoughts is an individual responsibility. To live differently than one is living now, one must think differently. Change the thought and the feeling changes immediately. After all, isn't what we feel the result of what we think?

A good case in point is the feeling of loneliness. How could anyone feel lonely on a planet of three billion inhabitants? A successful person is one who is willing to change his thinking to meet the demands of his goals.

No matter what element of society one chooses to focus upon, the element of change is ever present. Individuals, cities, laws, wealth, and thinking itself are all in a constant process of change. In order to conceive a future, one must perceive the present. One's ability to project the future is always a function of how one perceives the present in its historical context. One who dwells on the past loses the present. One who ignores the past, loses the future. One who understands the past gains the present and is competent to project a future. This again is one of the secrets of all who earn great wealth. They are the future because they are more competent at projecting it. They become leaders because they are the ones who change first.

It is the successful individual who is always able to best overcome any temporary difficulty because he knows it is just that — temporary. He knows things will change. He is always on the lookout for some way to change things to his own advantage. He is ever conscious that everything has a cyclic nature. He purposes to direct his efforts to take advantage of the cycles as a means of leveraging his way to success.

Market booms are a case in point. Much less thinking is required in a boom. It is far easier to be swept along with the impetus of the boom and raise prices along with everyone else. But what is lost in a boom is a sense of values. Toward the end the price picture has become so distorted that prices fail to mean much anymore. One gets caught up in a false sense of wealth. People come to the state of mind that they think the boom will go on forever. And yet, the end is imminent! All booms come to an end. And they usually end in a "bust." It is to a proper sense of values that people must return.

It is the successful thinker who is aware of such cycles and he is just the one who is probably going in the opposite direction of those caught up in a market boom. He is always the one who accurately anticipates the changes in things such as technology, habits, styles and so on. He is aware that economic disorder is like an epidemic. Once it starts, it accelerates with devastating rapidity. He has learned that in all market down swings, that it is the small business which is hit first. The larger concern is hit later, but the impact is always deeper.

Recovery is always slow or fast depending on which area of the market the boom is centered. There is always a slower recovery after a real estate speculation boom because of the huge capital investment in a slow moving commodity. Where prices can move quickly and the commodity is easily traded, recovery is usually much sooner.

A universal characteristic of all successful people is their respect for money. They learn the value of money because they have had to earn it. What one does with money is determined by how one views money. Money, like any other human value, is a responsibility. Treat it with disdain and money will take a speedy exit. Undermine its intrinsic characteristics and soon it will be devalued by everyone. But respect it, and all its noble purposes, and it will rise as a living monument to the culture it serves.

Money can never be the root of all evil since ethical considerations apply only to people. Morality can only be an issue of human action. And it is what we do with our money that makes the difference. Growth, of course, is the principle consideration. The kind that evolves from production. Destruction is its antithesis and when money is used for such purposes, its user is as evil as they come. All, both in the present and the future, must make themselves aware of what their money accomplishes. Getting rich as a by-product of human misery could hardly be considered successful living.

100

A common misconception is that money solves problems. It doesn't! All successful people who acquire wealth become aware of the many more problems that are connected with handling large sums of money. How does one protect it? In which investments will I keep from losing my shirt? The wise know that it is far more difficult to keep money than it is to get it.

Always remember that money is a flowing force. It moves in channels that are ever changing. Competition sees to that. And you can be sure that in the long run, money will always serve purposes that are good. If you doubt that, you need only check the history of nations that debased their money. They destroyed themselves! The word "debased" means, literally, they blocked out of their minds the knowledge of what they were doing. That is never a way to successful living.

Focus is a process of regulated selection of the contents of one's consciousness. One's spirit is the totality of one's thought processes. Consciousness is one and all differentiation of its aspects can only be for the purpose of understanding. Consciousness is a unity and to dichotomize it can only result in misconception. To know one's own mind is to know oneself and is a precondition to success. Self-knowledge is a prerequisite to self-control. To control anything requires an understanding of it. Self-control is essential to success. It is the first principle of success and the one upon which all others are founded.

To become successful one must develop a success consciousness. Success is a cumulative process that continues to attract more and more success factors. In the process of accumulation, it is the element of thinking around which everything else is centered. One has to become accomplished at successful thinking. It is the factor of trained thinking that is crucial in determining success. It is easy to see which kind of

101

thought is the most powerful.

Thinking IS living! And it is controlled thought that makes successful living possible. Success itself is a form of equilibrium. And balanced thought is always a product of integrated thought. The integrated thinker is one who is able to bring all the elements of his thought process to apply them to his goal.

Presuming that your goals are realistic, you have not failed if you have not attained them yet. You have simply acquired the knowledge of a preponderance of things that do not work in proportion to things that do work. In fact, there are no failures in the universe. There is only completion and non-completion. Atoms do not fail, they are reorganized. Cells do not fail, they are transformed. Human beings do not fail, they dissipate into nothingness.

You are the master of a galaxy of living organisms within your own body. Nature has exerted a tremendous effort to bring you where you are now. Right at this very moment you are being supported by a vast complexity of atoms, cells, and glands along with that marvelously integrated structure which is your brain. An array of natural forces such as gravity, electricity, and sunlight which are all on your side, supporting all that you do in your life. The universe is programmed with livingness. It is always successful. And it has programmed you to succeed. If you do not take advantage of your assets, you will not fail — you will simply disappear!

Action is the manifestation of all life. Mind and body are one. Thought is the leverage in all the actions of our life. Knowledge is the leverage in all thought. Never forget this: the only difference between a millionaire and a pauper is a little thinking. Money does not make the difference. The pauper merely accepts his condition in his own mind; and he probably blames the whole world for his poverty.

If you have goals that you want to achieve, get moving. Get

into action! Think, plan, work, and keep on moving. Problems are an excuse. There are no problems in the universe. What seems to be a problem is a question in the mind, moving on its way to reality — the answer. The universe itself is one infinite answer!

Challenge is the spice of all success. A goal, of itself, is a form of challenge. It is precisely the acceptance of challenge that launches one into action. It is one of the secrets of all who earn wealth. We all notice immediately the person who has accepted a challenge — he is busy! He is always accumulating, ever experimenting, and always striving to achieve his particular goal. It sets the course of his life. And if he reaches his goal, he becomes it — he IS it!

One of the hallmarks of a good salesman or a successful businessman is the ability to create value. All selling is creative whether the product is tangible or intangible. The tangible product was an idea before it was produced and all selling involves the selling of ideas. Creating value is doing something new, seeing new potentials, perhaps something that has never been achieved before.

Taking risks is something that everyone experiences on a daily basis. In just about every area of human activity there is an element of risk involved. This includes the routine but by force of habit we are not as conscious of the risk. It is when we step out and do something different that we become more aware of risk. Calculation then becomes the keynote. What differentiates the successful from the unsuccessful person is the factor of individuality. By individuality we mean the ability to think for oneself. This means to judge for oneself. High values always require the most independent thinking.

Society is a complex mechanism and leadership is the highest value of every culture. Dictators do not lead; they push. A dictator is the most unsuccessful person in the world. He is not a leader. He is a follower with a gun in his hand. He is the epitome of incompetence.

Competence is the measure of a leader. As we stated in the beginning, success and competence are equivalent.

We live our lives on a continuum and the levels of growth that we achieve are levels of success. Each time we reach a new plateau we add to the success of everyone else. The totality is what we call civilization. Chaos is its opposite.

Human life is an upward spiral on its way to wisdom. A salute to those who have gone before us and shown us a better way is a form of self-compliment; it is the wisdom of youth! It is success!

Biographies of
Self Made Millionaires

"The Biography of Millionaires"

W. Clement Stone

The life of W. Clement Stone is a "success story within a success story." Now chairman of Success Unlimited magazine, Stone has become the leader of the Positive Mental Attitude philosophy.

Although many a youth has had experience selling newspapers to make money, few are willing to endure and overcome the opposition that confronted W. Clement Stone. Having been thrown out of a restaurant several times because the proprietor thought he was annoying customers, Stone came back, and back, and back again. Finally, it was the customers themselves who came to his support because of his persistance, and Stone was allowed to continue selling his papers in the restaurant.

He began early to question himself on the things he was doing that would get sales and also on the things he thought were costing him sales. He would analyze himself and decide what he was going to do the next time.

His father having died when Stone was a child, Stone was raised by his mother who worked as a seamstress for many years. A hard working woman with an astute sense of business, she was to have a profound influence on Stone's life.

Young Clement was only in his teens when his mother took the money she had saved and invested it in an insurance agency of small means. The agency occupied a small office with very little furniture. Stone's mother became the agency's sales force; there was no one else. Her first day in the field resulted in no sales. A religious woman, she returned home and prayed before going to bed, and again in the morning before she started her day.

The next day she came home with forty-four sales. She had gone to the biggest bank in Detroit, and after selling one of the bank officers, proceeded to sell everyone in the building she could reach that day. Through her efforts, the small agency began to prosper.

Soon, Stone himself decided that he would try his hand at selling policies for his mother's agency. While only a junior in high school, and under the instruction of his mother, he set out for one of the office buildings in Detroit. By using self-motivators that he was later to incorporate in his PMA philosophy, he made two sales on his first day out.

Following his previous activity of self-analysis and self-motivation, Stone dug deep within himself and on his second day out, he doubled his first day's production. The third day he tripled it! On the first day out, in order to overcome being rejected again and again, Stone simply worked harder—he started to rush to get to the next prospect. He kept telling himself to "Do it now!".

During his time off from school and through summer vacation, Stone continued to sell the health-and-accident policies for his mother. His sales average steadily climbed. Finally, over some minor conflict at school, Stone came to the realization that he was making more money than the school principal. That was the end of school.

107

He went to work full time for his mother, and the number of policies he sold per day continued to rise. First thirty, then forty, and so on. Later, when he was age twenty, he opened his own agency in Chicago. He brought back fifty-four policies on his first day out.

He worked from city to city around Chicago and continued to reach higher and higher volumes until one day, he averaged one sale every four minutes. His total for the day was one hundred and twenty policies. Renewals had started to come in and there was no longer any doubt as to whether his agency would succeed.

Around the fourth year of selling for his own agency, Stone decided it was time to expand. Getting permission from insurance companies in other states to sell policies, he began a hiring campaign. His efforts reached out in all directions and within six years, his sales force grew to an army of over one thousand agents. His operation had now grown so large that he was doing business all over the country.

Then disaster struck! Depression. The number of agents working for him dwindled with the number of policies they were writing. What to do? Reaching within himself as in the past, Stone looked for answers to overcome the adversity with which he was now faced. With the morale of his sales force at its lowest ebb, his business reaching new lows, and a public thoroughly disillusioned by economic hardship, W. Clement Stone faced his situation as a challenge.

He gathered himself together, went back into the field and proved to the members at his organization that "Sales are contingent on the attitude of the salesman, not the prospect." Later, he was to incorporate this ideal in the sale of his success philosophy. The sales force of Combined Registry, Stone's agency, had in the meantime shrunk to 200 men.

Not having previously given that much attention to the

108

men in his organization, Stone now embarked on the effort of going to the various offices of his agency to bolster sales. He used bulletins filled with the PMA philosophy, worked with the men individually and in groups. Within a few years his 200 man sales force was writing more business than when 1,000 men were working with him. Stone was soon to become a millionaire.

Always looking out for new ways to grow, W. Clement Stone decided it was now time to have his own insurance company. By convincing the owners of an insurance company to loan HIM the money to buy the insurance company from them, Stone went into debt for around one and a half million dollars. Pennsylvania Casualty, the company he purchased, had ceased its sales operations because of economic woes. With its assets valued at 1.6 million dollars, Stone renamed the company the Combined Insurance Company of America. It was to grow into one of America's giants. Sales volume in the 70's was in the hundreds of millions. The sales force was to grow into thousands and a portion of the men were also to become millionaires themselves.

Always on the lookout for opportunity, W. Clement Stone diversified into other business enterprises. Book publishing had become one of his interests. Houses such as Appelton-Century-Crofts and Hawthorne Books were merged under the Stone umbrella.

The launching of Alberto-Culver into one of the cosmetic giants was also, in part, the effort of Stone. It was he who guaranteed the loan of around a half million dollars that enabled Leonard Lavin to lead Alberto-Culver in its rapid growth. The one quarter stock ownership given to Stone grew to some thirty million dollars in a few short years.

Horatio Alger stories had been one of Stone's major inspirations when he was a boy. The rags-to-riches episodes dominating the Alger's books were consumed by Stone along

109

with millions of other people at the time. Stone read them by the dozens.

To this day, Stone's first passion is the spreading of the Positive Mental Attitude philosophy. Critical of schools in that they do not teach people how to acquire wealth, Stone believes that wealth building can be learned like anything else. And who else is most likely to know?

Stone is, after all, the builder of a vast financial empire. His knowledge did not just jump out of things into his head. He had to learn them just as well as anyone else who acquired a fortune. And this is the basis of the PMA philosophy; "You can do it if you believe you can!".

In addition to acquiring publishing houses, W. Clement Stone turned to writing books in the 60's. Forming an alliance with Napoleon Hill, author of "Think and Grow Rich," the two men turned out a highly successful volume titled "Success Through a Positive Mental Attitude." The entire volume is steeped in principles that both men used in obtaining their wealth. Should a reader of this highly inspirational volume not acquire monetary riches, it is for certain he will acquire the wealth of character by adopting its principles.

In 1962 Stone added another fascinating volume to his penmanship. Even the title holds a guarantee—"The Success System That Never Fails." Will it work? Let us hope in humbleness, that we can all learn a few things from a man who has made around a half billion dollars!

W. Clement Stone has not rested on his laurels. He continues working full time, buying companies, and steadily increasing his net worth.

Aristotle Socrates Onassis

Greek Owner of Largest Tanker Fleet In the World

The study of what is usually called "Ancient Greece" is the study of the men and women who created the culture of that era. It is an exciting and rewarding adventure that never leaves one quite the same. Advancing forward about two thousand years to our own time, we meet another Greek who has dramatically changed the world in which we now live.

He is Aristotle Socrates Onassis.

His name alone packs so much power that one would almost expect him to become renowned. That is exactly what has happened.

Born in a country and at a time that was permeated with social conflict, suppression, war, and destruction, Onassis was to be shaped by many pressures and forces. He was, in turn, to change much of the world by the power he exerted from within himself.

The frequently changing political power under which he spent his youth and adolescence was to take its toll on the lives of his relatives, their fortunes, their way of life, and eventually cause Onassis to leave his homeland.

His mother died when he was six years old. From the ages of eight to twelve he lived under the threat of the ravages of a world war. At the age of sixteen, the Turkish invasion under Mustapha Kemal resulted in the confiscation of his home. Some of his relatives ecaped while others were confined; the unfortunate were summarily executed. His father was imprisoned as a "political" and was later to be executed.

Aristotle Socrates Onassis learned to bargain early. And he learned to bargain for that which is most precious—human life!

111

It was only four years after the end of a world war when the Turkish forces invaded and recaptured Onassis' home city of Smyrna. Having lost control of the city three years earlier to Greek forces, the Turks came down on the city with a vengeance. Smyrna became a slaughter-house!

Onassis survived the slaughter by quickly providing one thing—service. His life was eventually saved by the help he gave to two people,—a Turkish general and an American vice-consul stationed at the American compound in Smyrna. Both men liked Onassis. Through the American he was able to get releases for his step-mother and sisters from the detention camp where they were being held by the Turks. They were transported to safety on an American vessel. Release for his father was another matter, and the matter was money.

Greek prisoners were being executed daily without trial and it was only a matter of time before his father joined the dead. Onassis first marshalled together some of his father's Turkish business associates. Their combined protest against his father's execution delayed the inevitable for a time.

Onassis had acquired passes from both the Turk and the American so that he was able to visit his father in prison each day. One form of help that he had given the Turk and the American was the supply of liquor.

Because he was nearing the age of 17 and Turkish deportation decrees affected males over age 17, Onassis began to make his move to leave Smyrna. Stopping to see his father at the Turkish prison, Onassis was detained for questioning. He had been carrying secret messages in and out of the prison and knew that he must escape or be executed along with the others. During the questioning, the commandant was called away by headquarters, just long enough for Onassis to make his move. The guards had been used to seeing him come and go, so Onassis went; this time for good. The American vice-consul was his means of escape from Smyrna and the Turk

112

threat. He then joined his step-mother and sisters in Lesbos.

His father, however, was still in prison. It was decided among the remaining relatives at Lesbos that Aristotle Onassis was to be the one to go to Constantinople to purchase his father's release. This he accomplished. But there was one criticism made by the members of his family that was to take Onassis thousands of ocean miles away from Greece. Along with his father, they all thought he agreed to pay too much money for his father's release. Profoundly affected by their opinions, Aristotle left for Buenos Aires. He had decided that he would earn his fortune in Argentina and make up the money he had paid to the Turks for ransom.

Aristotle Onassis was seventeen years old when he arrived in Buenos Aires and it was like arriving in a new world. The city was quite modern compared to his home in Smyrna. The ravages of war were not to be found here. It was a thriving metropolis of two million people. Indeed, it was a new world. He took whatever work he could find for about the first year until he got a steady job with the telephone company. It was night work which left his days free to look for other opportunities. With steady (and overtime) work at the telephone company, the hardships of the first year now became a thing of the past.

Although there had been bitterness with his father over the high ransom paid for his father's release from Turkish prison, Onassis resumed correspondence. His father, now back in the tobacco business, suggested that he inquire about markets for Greek tobacco in Buenos Aires. After trying to work through the chain of command of a local tobacco dealer, Onassis went to the top by standing in front of the dealer's office door for about two weeks. The dealer, no longer being able to ignore Onassis' presence each day, asked him what he was doing. The next day Onassis had his first sale and drew a $500.00 commission. The tobacco orders not only continued, they grew larger.

He quit his job at the telephone company after about one year of tobacco trading and moved into a small hotel. Up to this time he had been mostly living in a boarding house.

He slept little. He traded in other commodities wherever he saw a chance for profit. He was always on the alert for an opportunity to make money.

He had purchased a cigarette company and borrowed the money to buy it. He used his own money for the collateral. In the years ahead he would duplicate this method whenever he could. He had also begun to buy Argentine tobacco for his cigarette company.

His income continued to rise with his many business activities. It was now six years since he had arrived in Buenos Aires and he had become a millionaire. Aristotle Socrates Onassis was only 23 years old.

Political bickering over trade treaties between Greece and Bulgaria put a stop to tobacco trading between Greece and Argentina. Onassis immediately sailed to Greece. He had been sending money to his relatives to help restore their lives and he was eagerly welcomed in Greece. The bonds between him and his father were again drawn closer.

A memorandum that he had started preparing before he left Argentina was now presented to the Greek government. Immunity to Argentina from the political conflict opened the way to the tobacco trade again and so Onassis sailed for Buenos Aires. But along with the grant of immunity, the Greek government had also made him envoy to Argentina. He was to hold his new status as consul general for six years and he learned much through the assignment. Many more doors opened to him as a result.

In the foregoing years, Onassis had developed a passion for classical music and had also learned to play the piano. He loved the works of Homer through which he had embodied the same spirit that had propelled Greeks two thousand years earlier to launch a cultural revolution that changed the face of the world. His self-assurance had grown steadily and he knew that he was to make his presence felt in the world.

By this time Onassis had expanded his trading activities to include grains, hides, and whale oil. He had already begun to take an interest in the shipping business and had resurrected a sunken vessel off the coast of Argentina, restored it to operating condition and sold it for an enormous profit.

Shortly after he had returned to Buenos Aires, economic depression was taking its toll in one country after another. The 29 crash on Wall Street did not hit Argentine immediately, but as the depression deepened, Argentina was not exempt. Most of the shipping companies that did not go bankrupt were floundering. With no cargoes, their ships idle, and income at a severe low, the future did not look promising.

Aristotle Onassis saw the depression as an opportunity to go into the shipping business. Knowing there would be economic recovery, he made two trips to Europe to promote his tobacco business. He learned much about shipping wherever he went. With idle ships everywhere, they could be obtained at very low prices. Onassis also reasoned in favor of larger ships because their tonnage capacity held the potential of higher profits. He finally purchased six freighters in London and left them in mothballs for about two more years. As the world economy started to show signs of recovery he activated his vessels one at a time. Soon after that his fleet was showing higher profits than his competitors. He also moved the registration of his ships to Panama and Greece in order to avoid taxes and political regulations. He had purchased his old freighters at bargain prices and his investment was now paying off handsomely.

He had also begun to see that oil would replace coal as the power source of the world. Now he wanted new ships—tankers. Big ones! They made more money. "Ariston" was launched in 1938 and she was the largest tanker in the world. Two more giant tankers were launched soon after the "Ariston." Onassis was now becoming very rich.

Then suddenly things changed. Adolph Hitler smashed through Poland, dealing a shock to the world. Aristotle's new tankers were docked in the neutral ports of Scandinavian countries and all his efforts were not enough to get them released. All three of his giant new tankers were to sit idle for the remainder of the war. A second blow came with the Italian entry into the war which brought formerly neutral Greece into the conflict. The German occupation of Greece ended Aristotle's source of Balkan tobacco. After going to the United States to buy more ships and failing, Onassis returned to Buenos Aires to reorganize.

Onassis did arrange to purchase tobacco from other South American countries, although it was not of the high quality that he had been importing from Greece. He still had the six ships he had purchased in London. He was able to generate a high volume of income from these six vessels alone. He entered other lesser ventures during the war which were profitable, but had to wait until the war was over to continue his plans for bigger operations.

When the war ended, Onassis moved his headquarters to New York City. He had outgrown Buenos Aires and Europe was in shambles. The big money was in the United States. Shipbuilding had come to a halt and many American vessels used in the war effort were due to be sold to private companies. Onassis was looking for bargains and went after them. He was blocked out of being able to buy any of the 100 ships allocated to Greek ship owners. To overcome this setback he offered to pay around nine million dollars cash for

116

sixteen ships. And as usual, he borrowed the money to finance the purchase rather than tie up his own capital. He was busy arranging cargoes for the additional sixteen ships at the same time he was arranging the financing. Onassis was the first among the Greek ship owners to get New York City bank financing but the others were not slow in following his example.

The three largest tankers in the world that were held in Scandinavian ports for the duration of the war had been released and were back in operation. They were still owned by Onassis.

Onassis was now ready to swing into operation with his masterplan—the supertanker!

What occurred next was phenomenal. After meeting and overcoming one obstacle on top of another, with engineers claiming that demand for oil would never be great enough to fill such a huge ship, having to convince reluctant ship-builders to take on such a project after a string of negotiations extending over months Aristotle Socrates Onassis now had five supertankers under construction!

The cost? Forty million dollars!

Who financed it? Not Onassis. He used his shipping contracts with American oil companies as collateral!

What did he do next? He looked for more ships to buy! And later, he would build even larger supertankers.

High prices for whale oil were an attractive stimulant to Onassis. The pre-war dominance of the Norwegians in the whaling industry had changed with the destruction of Norwegian fleets during the war. Purchasing seventeen Canadian corvettes, he converted them into killer boats. Converting one of his surplus American T2 tankers into a flagship, he now had the finest whaling fleet in the world.

Conversion of ships in post-war Germany was permitted but construction was not. Refabrication of German yards was also attractive because of German competence in ship building. There were many workers available as Germany was still in ruins. Onassis was to play a major role in reviving the German economy. The eighteen ship conversion was to be done in Germany. In time, the total commitment made to German yards would reach approximately one hundred million dollars—the largest figure in German history. Later on, the German yards would build even bigger supertankers for Onassis.

By 1953, Onassis had the largest tanker fleet in the world which now consisted of around 100 ships. And with the launching of the Tina Onassis, he had the largest tanker in the world.

The following year he received delivery of the Christina, the largest yacht in the world. It also was the most luxurious. In time, the yacht was to become his headquarters.

By quickly obtaining shares of the corporation that owned the Monte Carlo casino in Monaco; he gained control. Moving his headquarters into the Sporting Club and attracting investments to the principality of Monaco, it became one of the finest resorts in the world.

Although Onassis would have to fight many legal battles, have his own private war with the goverment of Peru, endure a boycott of American oil companies, and compete with competent rivals in the supertanker industry, in almost every case he would end up much richer than before.

The American people got their first widely publicised introduction to Aristotle Onassis when he married Jackie Kennedy, widow of former president John F. Kennedy.

Onassis continued to be one of the most fascinating figures in the world, until he died in 1976 at age 70, leaving behind a remarkable legacy of success and accomplishment.

Ray Kroc

Founder of "McDonald's"

Almost everyone in America has eaten a hamburger and french fries at one time or another. But to become rich selling them became the dream of Ray Kroc, the promoter of McDonald's Hamburger chain.

Ray Kroc, at age 17, worked at a soda fountain while in school. Saving his money, he went into the music store business, his first. The business did poorly and Ray sold out. He sold coffee beans and also sold novelties door-to-door. He worked as a cashier for awhile.

As a student in school, Ray was highly attracted to debating classes. He did not care for reading much and disliked the slow progress of school. Ray was more of a man of action.

Always a dreamer, Ray was constantly imagining himself in different situations and figuring out what he would do. He was even called Danny Dreamer.

But he loved work and worked at something whenever possible. Later, he was to say that "work is the hamburger in the meat of life."

He learned to play the piano as a child and used his musical ability to supplement his income as a salesman more than once. He even played in a bordello for one night but never went back when he found out what it was. Taking to the piano naturally, he played at dime-a-dance pavillions, on a ferry boat, and also in an illegal club during prohibition. Having to share the tips, most of which he generated, he soon learned that by handling things differently, he could make more money by playing special requests and by playing serenading duos with the violinist when the rest of the band was on break.

Playing the piano for radio stations also brought him into

the position of interviewing different people for the shows. Two men he hired were later to become the famous "Amos and Andy."

Ray started selling paper cups for Lilly Cups when he was age 20, the same year he married his first wife Ethel. It was to be three years later before Ray started to make his mark as a paper cup salesman. Since the paper cup business was slow in the north during winter, Ray would go to Florida in search of other work. He sold underwater property in the 20's real estate boom in Florida and worked difficult hours at night playing the piano. At age 23, he purchased his first new car because of his success selling paper cups.

Ray's father died in 1930 after losing his holdings in the real estate speculation boom that ended in the 29 crash. This was the same year that Ray had captured his first large account, the Walgreen Drug Stores chain. From this account he went on to close sales at U.S. Steel, creameries, and closed accounts at Swift and Armour.

The merger of Lilly and Tulip cup companies in 1929 was an opportunity that Ray had seen; he had more lines to sell. He had also become salesmanager with around fifteen men working under him. He was to delight in seeing his men learn the ropes and become good salesmen.

Ray was to experience many detours before taking off with McDonald's, but he treated all of them as learning phases. The paper cup business led him into the Multimixer business which eventually led to McDonald's Hamburgers.

In his paper cup sales travels he had encountered a man named Earl Prince who had opened what were called Prince Castle ice cream parlors. It was Prince who invented the Multimixer. Seeing the opportunity of selling Multimixers all over the country, Kroc immediately went to work. Two large obstacles were to stand in his way to success in selling Multimixers. One was the sixty-eight thousand dollar buyout price to get exclusive distributor rights for Multimixer. Overcoming this adversity was to pay off later in his dealings in running McDonalds. Although World War II had temporarily ended his Multimixer business because copper was being used for the war effort, Ray sold a malted milk product and managed to pay off his debt. When the war ended, Ray went back to selling Multimixers and his business soon started rolling.

Five thousand multimixers a year was a good year for him and one year he sold eight thousand. Generating a large volume of business brought to him his first and long time business associate, June Martiono. Ray desparately needed a bookkeeper and even though June had no bookkeeping experience, he hired her basing his choice on the presence of her character. June was later to become secretary and treasurer of McDonalds.

It was in the early 50's that Ray Kroc saw that he had to find a new product to sell. Multimixer sales were no longer booming.

And it was the people who had been calling him to buy Multimixers because of the ones that they had seen in operation in a take-out restaurant in California that led Ray eventually to the McDonald's store there. Taking off for San Bernardino, a semi-desert town, Kroc was not expecting the experience that was soon to propel him to tremendous business success. He went to find out why he was getting so many Multimixer referrals from this one location.

What he found was opportunity. But it was his keen business sense that enabled him to see it.

The year was 1954. Ray Kroc was 52 years old. He was still "green and growing" as he calls it.

Two brothers, Mac and Dick McDonald had converted a conventional, yet successful, restaurant to a take-out restaurant. The new store was a masterpiece of simplicity and efficiency. Their only products, hamburgers and cheeseburgers, were so delicious that they drew all kinds of people from everywhere. The hamburgers were 15¢! The smoothness, cleanliness, and rapid service of the whole operation so impressed Kroc that he immediately entered into a leasing arrangement with the McDonald brothers.

The "Golden Arches" of McDonalds which had been installed at the first store were later to be seen by millions of people all over the world. And the French fries, sold by the McDonalds that were so outstanding in taste, were also to be eaten by those same people.

Returning to his home in Illinois, Ray set up his first store in Des Plaines. It was here that he was to have to overcome many difficulties before making the store successful. One of the difficulties was ridicule. He was even accused of being crazy. He also had to overcome the difficulty of duplicating the McDonald French fry; this alone took three months!

Finally the store started to show a profit and Ray was by this time paying attention to the potential of opening more McDonald stores. The following year, he opened three more stores in California and eight more were opened in 1956.

When Harry Sonneborn, an expert in finance, joined forces with Ray Kroc, things really began to move. Their association gave birth to the Franchise Realty Corporation which was later to vault the McDonald chain to unprecedented success. In 1957, twenty-five more stores were opened.

Always a perfectionist, Ray Kroc viewed executive ability as measured by the fewest mistakes. He also knew that to hire a man to do a job meant to get out of the way and let him do it. Fred Turner now joined the Kroc team and was destined to head up operations.

"Quality, Service, Cleanliness and Value (QSV & C) had become one of the success formulas of the McDonald stores and it was to multiply itself many times over.

Dealing with everything from wasted seconds in handling hamburger buns, the proper amount of hamburger patties to be in one stack, more efficient systems of receiving deliveries, eventual personality clashes, mechanic's liens, financing problems, a costly divorce, and other difficulties, Ray Kroc moved on. Although the McDonald's stores at last count had passed four thousand, Ray, still a dreamer, is looking toward a figure of ten thousand stores. McDonald's has also passed the one billion dollar gross income mark.

Ray Kroc, viewing his success as his tribute to free enterprise, went on to save a baseball team for the city of San Diego. This he did through the purchase of the Padres when he was in his early 70's. Yet, he still considers himself as "green and growing"!

Although there have been changes in personnel, changes in store architecture, and additions to the McDonald menu, the essential principles of McDonald operations are mostly the same. When fighting competition he stresses strength and using one's mind to always stay in front. Always a salesman and promoter, Ray still believes that "There's almost nothing you can't accomplish if you set your mind to it."

Work is still his play.

Joe Sugarman

Founder of JS & A Inc.

From trade show publication to mail order sales, Joe Sugarman, of JS & A Group, Inc., is another success story that demonstrates that people can still make it big. At age 42, in 1980, Sugarman added another dimension to his career by writing a book titled "Success Forces."

Born in 1938, Joe Sugarman had his first start in a small printing business. His father, also a printer, had helped him get started. Joe was able to pay back the money for the equipment from the income he derived from printing.

His favorite activity in grammar school had been writing and he learned early to amuse his classmates with humor. He continued his writing in high school where he began to publish his own paper because he disliked the school paper. Organizing around himself the best writers in the school, the paper became a success. He had also become sports photographer for the school and was therefore able to include photographs in the paper.

Majoring in Journalism, Joe entered the University of Illinois. Taking a summer vacation in Florida convinced him to continue his schooling there. He changed his major to Electrical Engineering as a compromise to his father but writing was still his first passion. After two years in Florida he went to New York to help out in his father's printing business.

On the suggestion of his father Joe next tried a trade show promotion at the New York Trade Show Building. He hired a sixty-five year old actor to help him with the booking because he was only twenty years old and thought the distinguished appearance of the actor would boost his sales. It worked! Spectra 59, as the show was titled, was soon sold out.

Returning to college as a far more serious student because

124

of his taste of the business world, Joe's grades immediately improved. He trimmed his social activities.

Getting inspiration from the success of Neil Sedaka, a rock singer, Sugarman next turned to song writing. He was after a hit record and cranked out numbers with titles such as, "Santa's Got a Problem," "Is It Chilly in Chile during Christmas," and the novelty "Mudder Goose." Getting rejections from one recording company after another, Joe next turned to a black recording company. On the prodding of the producer, Joe invested along with his efforts around three thousand dollars in the production of "Mudder Goose." It was a flop.

The Berlin crisis ended Joe's college career when he was drafted into the army and trained to be an undercover agent for army intelligence. Working in Germany on various assignments, Joe was eventually discharged there. Having met some of his father's European business associates who wanted to open a ski-lift company in the United States, Joe returned to America to establish Ski-Lift International in 1965. Joe was now twenty-seven years old.

Again, Sugarman turned to writing by applying his skills to the sales literature for Ski lift. Some of the companies that purchased ski lifts for their resorts, in turn, hired Joe to help with their advertising. Because of conflicts with the major stockholders of Ski-Lift, Joe soon left the company. But by this time his confidence had grown in his advertising penmanship, and he formed his own advertising agency.

Around this time the Batman fad was being used by merchandisers to sell anything from T-shirts to toys. Credit cards sales were also experiencing rapid growth. "Why not a Batman Credit Card?," thought Joe. After making the necessary contacts, a quarter of a million cards were made, radio and printing promotions were lined up, and a former friend moved to Chicago to help with sale of Batman Credit Cards, Sugarman was ready to roll. Only one thing was missing; the contract and license to sell the card. It was to be another twelve years before he obtained a release and then it was too late. The Batman fad had faded. Joe was broke, in debt, and had 250,000 Batman cards on his hands.

His next promotion, in 1966, a plastic paddle ball game which he named the Teeny Bopper. Around it he decided to form a club which he named the Great Teeny Bopper Society. Using radio taped ads, memberships started to roll in. He then decided to go big by launching a promotion using a discount store, members of the Grand-mothers Club of Chicago as models, and more radio spot ads. However, a few hours before Kick-off, a tornado struck, and wiped out the whole promotion.

All the while, Sugarman was using his advertising writing to pay the bills to keep himself and family in food and shelter. In each promotion effort he had increased his ad writing skills and was still learning.

He next tried teen-club and rock group promotion. His efforts here led eventually to writing sales literature for All-Tapes, a company that distributed tape recordings of rock singers. Losing that account in the 1970 recession, Joe began prospecting for new clients. He had also been doing advertising promotions for various Chicago politicians with above average success.

It was in 1971 while Joe Sugarman was working for Thomas Foran's gubernatorial campaign that he came across the electronic pocket calculator that was to change his life. Noticing the calculator being used by one of the campaign assistants, Joe was allowed to take the calculator home and try it. He saw its advantages instantly. Seeing an ad in Business Week magazine for another calculator at a much lower price, he tracked down Craig Corporation, who produced the calculator.

Drawing in one of his former associates from the rock singer promotions, they formed a small investment alliance and tried to sell the calculator on a direct mail basis. Although they lost money on the first venture, they learned that selection of the right mailing lists was important.

By this time Joe had learned that each time he thought something was going to be a smashing success, it was usually a flop. Knowing that not being successful with the calculator sale would probably mean a serious setback from which it would take a long time to recover, Joe, confused, sought advice from a former friend who ran a letter service. Under the advice of Harvey Wagley of United Letter Service, mailing lists were purchased and with the necessary preparations, the second direct mail promotion was executed in January of 1972.

First a trickle, and then a Flood of orders started to roll in. The mail out was a success!

Meanwhile, his home had become a factory for shipping calculator orders. Calculator prices were starting to drop and Joe sensed that he must try to reach the largest number of potential customers as quickly as possible. Trickles of competition were starting to emerge.

Basing his next move on the view that a reader, if interested enough in a product, would go all the way through a lengthy ad, Sugarman decided to advertise in the Wall Street Journal. The ad appeared on February 28, 1972 and with it, orders for the Craig calculator rolled in. He made twenty-thousand dollars in the first ten days.

He also learned that the most successful ads were those that were the most descriptive, pointing out advantages and disadvantages. Later, he ran an advertisement titled "The Truth About Pocket Calculators" in which he described not only the features of various calculators, but also the different places where people could buy them. He also included a reference to another ad he had in the same paper in which he was offering five competitively priced calculators for sale. The descriptive honesty in "Truth" advertisement brought another deluge of orders and in a few weeks sales volume hit a quarter of a million dollars.

It was during the calculator promotion that Joe learned one of the essentials of all successful businesses: service, and more service and better service, produces more customers.

His next marketing innovation was the introduction of the 800 toll free number as a device for quickly getting orders. Again the business swarmed in! People had been using their credit cards for ordering calculators for a year. Using the 800 toll free number had made it much easier to place an order. It was Joe Sugarman who augmented the explosion of WATS line usage.

Joe's next promotion effort was destined to teach him a very serious business principle—concentration. Trying to take advantage of the Watergate political scandal, he and an associate invented a Watergate Scandal Game. However, immediately after funds were invested in the production of the game, adverse television interviews brought sales to a halt. Despite the money lost, Joe learned the necessity of focusing on his successful company, JS & A.

Although his Wall Street Journal ads gave the impression of a billion-dollar corporation, Sugarman and associates were still operating out of his basement. But in early 1974, having outgrown the use of his home as a business headquarters, the operation was moved to a converted gasoline station. Again, through the use of innovative ads and bringing in even much larger calculator orders, they were soon forced to relocate to larger quarters in an industrial park.

Joe's recent book *Success Forces* outlines the dynamic motivations that made him a winner.

Edwin H. Land

Inventor of the Polaroid Land Camera

Born in the 19th century, photography was the applied result of centuries of scientific effort. Chemistry, mechanics, optics, and mathematics are all wrapped up in that little package that we today call a camera.

Most of us have had the opportunity to have been photographed with a Polaroid camera by now. However, back of the picture that we hold in our hand is the life of a very unique man.

Edwin H. Land was seventeen years old when he first got the idea of producing polaroid filters. The impetus that propelled him on a new course for the rest of his life was an experience common to many people at the time. The event was the glare of automobile headlights in his eyes. His idea was to eliminate the glare by polarizing the light.

Land was a university student at the time and had already been studying science. He began a systematic search for all the material he could find that explained the properties of polarizing substances. He combed libraries and any other source he could find that dealt with the subject.

He conducted private experiments for two years before he perfected his first polarizing sheets. His application for a patent was made in 1928 when Land was only age 19.

He had dropped out of school for two years so that he could devote all of his time to research and the development of functional polarizing sheets. Although he had not as yet developed them to the point of practical application, the sheets were functional.

When he returned to Harvard University the following year, he was awarded research facilities after he displayed his invention to the science faculty. He continued his studies at Harvard for another three years before finally deciding to again devote himself fully to the development of his work. It was 1932 and Land was 23 years old.

He formed Land-Wheelright Laboratories the same year with George W. Wheelright, one of Harvard's physics instructors. The first practical materials in sheet form were developed and further research and development was continued for the next five years until the Polaroid Corporation was founded by Land in 1937.

Capitalization of $375,000.00 was provided by a group of Wall Street investors to whom Land had demonstrated his invention. A patent had been awarded to him three years earlier in 1934. From 1937 to 1941, a variety of products employing polarizing sheets were sold by the new corporation. They ranged from sunglasses to filters used in scientific laboratories. Sales reached the $1,000,000.00 mark in 1941, four years after the corporation was founded.

What is unique in the case of Land's association with Polaroid is the fact that Land is a scientist. It is rare indeed for a scientist to head up a major corporation.

The original motivation of the investors who backed Land was the application of polarization filters to automobile headlights and windshields. The intervention of the Second World War from 1941 to 1945 diverted most of Polaroid's efforts to the production of military optics. After the war automobile applications again became the focus.

1947 was a crucial year for Edwin Land and Polaroid. Sales had plummeted from a 1945 high of $17,000,000 to $1,500,000. Losses for the year totaled $2,000,000. Detroit rejected the automobile application even though all tests had shown favorable results. However, there was one highlight; the sixty-second camera was now functional.

Land had been the only Polaroid science and engineering

specialist to date. Now engineers William J. McCune and Otto Wolf accepted the challenge of getting the camera into production. Both were to make important engineering improvements. J. Harold Booth and Robert S. Casselman were assigned to promotion and sales.

It was not until late 1948 that the camera was offered for sale. A trial run was made in a Boston department store and the camera supply was quickly sold out. Subsequent trials were repeat sellouts and mass distribution was begun.

1949 sales rose to around $7,000,000, most of which was from camera and film sales. In the following five years, film-fading problems had to be dealt with and were eventually solved.

Hollywood, in 1953, began showing three-dimensional color movies using the Vectograph method first presented by Polaroid at the 1939 World's Fair. Because of the two-projector synchronization problems, the 3-D affair only lasted one year. But Polaroid had grossed over five million dollars in viewing glasses alone.

Two new film speeds were added in 1955 and sales increased an average of thirty-six percent for the next three years. Subsequent development of film in the following years drove sales much higher. Color photography was introduced around 1960.

By 1968, camera sales had risen to $400,000,000. The first year of Land camera sales was around $5,000,000. Polaroid has continued to rise and surpass the sales of other camera companies.

Edwin Land has also been very active in developing methods to increase the creativity of Polaroid's employees. Believing creativity is not the monopoly of the scientist alone, Land uses the methods of delegation and persuasion in management. He prefers to thoughtfully guide his company by inspiration.

Edwin Land's methods are "the proof of the pudding." The success of Polaroid in the last twenty-five years is now history. The meteoric growth of Polaroid since 1955 once again proves that people are the power behind any successful business. Land has continued to surround himself with competence and the many additions to the Polaroid Land Camera, new developments in film, and other Polaroid products have all contributed to Polaroid's phenomenal rise.

The income of a corporation fluctuates like the income of an individual. Since a corporation is composed of individuals, in all cases it is the thinking that is done by each individual that makes the difference. Land originally conceived the idea of the camera in 1944 when his young daughter asked why it took so long to see a photograph after a picture was taken. From that question which moved through the mind of a creative genius has come a useful product that has touched the lives of millions of people. That question was to occupy Land's valuable spare time for the next three years.

When he had finally produced a functional camera in 1947, the only issue remaining was to mass produce it. The important thing to Polaroid at that time was that the company needed something badly to turn the tide. Today, not only has the Land camera produced employment for thousands of people, it has also made Land and a number of others very wealthy. The rapid results of the camera have greatly aided in scientific and technological research. Most of all, however, is that it has added a little more happiness to the lives of millions.

Edwin Land, a scientist, a dreamer, and yet a man of accomplishment has added to man's knowledge and enriched the lives of millions through his inventions.

CONSTANCE BOUCHER
Founder of Determined Productions

Determined Productions became the name of the company that vaulted Constance Boucher to the status of millionairess. Today her creations and promotions are sold in many parts of the world.

Connie Boucher has been interested in business since childhood. Always making and building something, one of her first earning ventures was fixing hair for women in her neighborhood.

Connie learned the art of saleswomanship while she was a high school student. Working in many sections of a department store, she sold everything from needles to gloves. She displayed an enthusiasm that was contagious and, in most cases, she out-sold her co-workers.

Always of a creative nature, Connie later obtained work in interior-design shops, and did window displays for department stores. She had taken art classes in school and grew to consider her work as fun. Designing a window display for one of the Joseph Magnin stores, Connie got the idea for her first business venture. She was doing charitable work, at the same time, to help raise funds for the Children's Home Society. The charity group had decided to use Noah's Ark as the theme for their promotion activities. Connie was even successful at selling the Coast Guard on hauling an old barge from another city; she wanted to make everything as realistic as possible. She had also designed a Noah's Ark coloring book for children as a means of raising addition funds for the Children's Home. Getting Magnins and other stores to sell the coloring book to help out with the charity drive, Connie began to notice the popularity of the book. It was then that she recognized the business potential.

"Winnie-the-Pooh" had been one of Connie's favorite

literary experiences as a child. The "Pooh" illustrations, she decided, would make excellent material for the next coloring book. James Young, another Magnin employee, joined her efforts and suggested that the next book be increased to a larger than usual size. After buying the rights (for $500) to use "Winnie-the-Pooh" illustrations, a 15" x 18" "Pooh" coloring book was published. Connie and her husband had obtained funds for publication by mortgaging their homes. Yet she had not even sold her first order when the book went into production.

Her husband had suggested to her that the only thing she had going for herself was determination; this was the foundation of what was to become her new company — Determined Productions, Incorporated.

Connie was a believer in the idea that if one wanted to do something badly enough, the best thing was to just go ahead and do it! Although she was only able to place about six books in each of the first stores she contacted, the books were quickly sold out and she received orders for more. Within six months, 52,000 copies were sold, netting $40,000 to the fledgling Determined Productions.

More coloring books followed; "The Wind in the Willows," "Alice In Wonderland," and "The Wizard of Oz." Looking for avenues of growth, Connie expanded her promotions to other cities by contacting people who were advertised distributors. Two of the distributors were high power saleswomen and orders from distant cities flowed in.

Connie obtained promotions through Life and Look magazines by getting them to do stories on what she called "Pooh Parties." "Pooh" characters and fixtures were created on a tract of land, children were invited, and Life magazine provided three page coverage on the activities.

Although there were a few "character" products on the market at the time (the 1960s), the range was limited. On a visit to Europe, Connie had noticed that the novelty-gift business was more active than in America. Sensing that the novelty-gift business in America was due for considerable growth, she decided to go after the characters in the "Peanuts" comic strip. Her thinking on both issues was soon to be proven correct.

With James Young as full time art director, Connie and Determined Productions began to roll out "Peanuts" products. "Snoopy" stuffed animals, clothes, and toys were sold everywhere. Watches, sleeping bags, and shirts bearing the "Snoopy" emblem became commonplace. Even the Japanese became "Snoopyized." Determined Productions reaped millions from the venture, and it was only the beginning.

A royalty arrangement had been worked out with United Features Syndicate, the owners of the rights, to use the characters of Charles Schultz' "Peanuts" comic strip. The agreement provided that Determined could contract with other firms to make products with "Peanuts" characters on them. J.P. Stevens, a linen manufacturer, is reported to have sold $10,000,000 worth of "Peanuts" bedding in one year; a record for any single pattern sale.

Now located in San Francisco, California, Determined Productions has branched out into other lines. A restaurant, television, and motion pictures are being considered. Offices and syndications have been established as far away as Tokyo, Switzerland, and Hong Kong.

A closely held corporation, Determined Productions does not release sales figures. However, it has been reported (by an independent financial service) that Determined Productions volume has now reached twenty million dollars in annual sales.

Constance Boucher, energetic, organized, full of new ideas, and now a millionairess, says that she will not quit "... until I can't navigate."

JANET ESTY
Founder of Neomed

Another "newly arrived" among the millionairess class is Janet Esty of Boulder, Colorado. Lifted up from years of struggle at trying to survive and getting an education simultaneously, Janet has become prosperous on two fronts — medicine and electronics.

A self-supporting and self-made college graduate, she was not able to complete graduate school to become a surgeon. She held various jobs until graduating from college and since then has worked as a junior scientist, a technical writer and a medical writer. It was not until March of 1971 that Janet was able to establish her own business.

Neomed, the name of her new company, was founded by Janet and two of her former male associates. The three of them had been working for the same electronics firm in Boulder, Colorado when they decided to strike out on their own. Within the first two years, both men separated from the company, leaving Janet as President and sole officer.

Neomed's principal product was an electronic surgical knife that is used to burn through tissue, thus replacing the commonly used scalpel. Coagulating and cauterizing features are by-products of the electronic device. An electronic generator is used with the knife to supply the requisite electrical power.

The beginning phases of a business are the toughest and it was during this period that Janet noticed the most radical changes within herself. Taking greater control of everything, including herself, all unnecessary expenses were eliminated. The number of hours she had to work did not matter; she loved her work. Survival for the neophite company was her major concern.

The first order for two hundred generators was finally

secured. Since the generator sold for $2,500, this meant that she now had a commitment of around one-half million dollars. In the following years, Neomed would receive orders for thousands of generators, but it was the first order that was to launch the new enterprise.

Janet Esty, now around age forty, has since expanded Neomed's products to over fifty lines. The number of employees has steadily grown to meet the demands of the business generated by around sixty sales representatives working in the United States and abroad. Today, the line-up of Neomed customers ranges from Scripps Institute in La Jolla, California to Massachusetts General Hospital.

Totally committed to her work and the success of Neomed, Janet Esty has no qualms about replacing department heads for more efficient personnel. Organized and meticulous about detail, she is proud to send out all of Neomed's products with "The Finest in Electrosurgery" stamped on shipping cartons. Neomed is her life and has been the lever that has raised Janet Esty to the level of self-made millionairess.

DOTTIE WALTERS

One night in 1948, Dorothy Walters' husband came home from his dry cleaning establishment, sad and crushed. His business was on the verge of collapsing and everything they had worked for could be wiped out.

Dottie asked Bob only one question; "Bob, can you hold on for one more month?" He said he would try.

Turning to the Bible, Dottie read the tale of the widow who, despairing of losing her two sons into slavery, asked Elisha, "What can I do?"

The sage answered: "What hast thou in thy house?" The widow only had a little oil, but she greatly prospered by selling it to her friends and neighbors. She then turned to story of the "talents." What talent did she possess.

In 1948 Dottie Walters was a very young housewife with two little babies. What treasure had she that people would purchase? How could she multiply her "talent" in this time of financial crisis?

The Biblical words, "For unto every one that hath shall be given, and he shall have abundance," gave her a new vision of what she must do.

In high school Dottie had written a column for the school paper. She decided on a course of action. "This is my one talent," she declared.

The next day she pushed her two babies downtown in a

Taylor Tot to a weekly newspaper office. She talked a hard-nosed publisher into selling her an advertising column on credit.

Then, with her babies still in tow, Dottie called on local merchants in hopes of selling them ad space. She was shy and more than a little scared, but she persisted. Her "talent" began multiplying, until one of her sponsors—a garage man—told her, "Why don't you start a hospitality hostess service?"

Dottie thought it over and decided why not give it a go. She purchased a Model A Ford for $50. She decorated a large basket with flowers and bows. Inside there were such items as food, candy, maps of the town, coupon booklets and other literature. She then would proceed, with her two children with her, to the addresses of new arrivals in Baldwin Park, California. "Good morning, my name is Dottie Walters. I'm here to welcome you to Baldwin Park."

Soon Dottie was making 100 or more calls monthly. Each merchant who subscribed to her service paid a fixed amount for each call she made. In time she had to hire other women to help her with her rapidly expanding business. Husband Bob soon sold his dry cleaning business and joined Dottie in her growing venture.

Today Dottie Walters' Hospitality Hostess Service welcomes 5,000 new residents to Southern California each month. She serves an area known as the "Golden Triangle"—from Los Angeles to San Diego.

Dottie has also authored several books on success and

motivational subjects, including the best-selling "The Selling Power of a Woman" (published by Frederick Fell). She also has become one of the most sought after women speakers in the world. A member and former officer of the National Speakers Association, Dottie has spoken at motivational rallies worldwide, often sharing the platform with the most famous speakers in the world (Norman Vincent Peale, Art Linkletter, etc.). She also publishes a lively newsletter for public speakers, and those who wish to become speakers, called "Sharing Ideas Among Professional Speakers."

Dottie Walters is proof positive of what any woman (or man) can do with the help of faith, desire and determination.

Note: If you would like to receive literature on Dottie Walters books, tapes or newsletter, write: Dottie Walters, Royal CBS Publishing, 600 West Foothill Blvd., Glendora, CA 91740.

THE DISCOUNT BROKER

When he was 10 or 11, Charles ("Chuck") Schwab, 45, raised chickens in his parents' yard in Woodland, CA. "I'd take the chickens and the eggs and sell them door to door," he recalls. "It was a small enterprise—less than $100 million."

Schwab can afford to belittle his earlier entrepreneurial effort. He is the founder and head of Charles Schwab & Co., the nation's largest discount brokerage house. Profits in its most recent fiscal year were more than $3 million.

Schwab's personal worth jumped substantially in 1983 when he sold out to Bank of America. That sale netted him about 15 million dollars.

Schwab started his brokerage house in 1971. It struggled along until, in April 1974, the brokerage business was deregulated. Instead of the rigid rate structure that had been in effect, brokers could charge what they wanted. Schwab moved fast. He offered no-frills trading services, minus the research and hand-holding available from other brokers, at discounts that averaged 50%.

Industry experts were skeptical. They argued that investors had to be sold stocks by brokers—that people tended not to buy on their own initiative. Other brokers were outright hostile. Schwab found himself fighting to get seats on several stock exchanges. He spent hours combating rumors, apparently spread by rival firms, that his company was going out of business. Banks, influenced by the rumors, wouldn't lend to him, so Schwab had to pass the hat among family and friends. Office space was peculiarly hard to come by—big brokers apparently were telling landlords that they would pull out of buildings if they rented to Schwab. Today his firm has offices in more than 50 U.S. cities.

They recently leased 15 floors of a highrise office building in San Francisco, so obviously they are confident that the future for the business is very bright.

Schwab lives quietly with his wife and two of their five children (the others are grown) in a refurbished turn-of-the-century house in San Francisco's South Bay area. He is a tennis player, a duck hunter and an enthusiastic reader. Schwab & Co. just opened its first overseas office, in Hong Kong.

THE LONG-DISTANCE MAN

No one, but no one, had ever taken on Ma Bell and survived to brag about it. So, in 1968, William McGowan decided to try. Says he: "The fact that it had never been done before made the idea all the more irresistible."

McGowan, 56, is the founder and head of MCI Communications Corp., and the idea was to compete with the world's largest company in the lucrative long-distance telephone market. And compete he has. MCI's revenues for 1983 are expected to top $1 billion. McGowan's stock alone is worth an estimated $96 million. He has earned "bragging rights."

McGowan was a self-employed management consultant when he began MCI with only $50,000 of his own money. He used it to buy the rights to the name of Microwave Communications Inc., a dormant Chicago firm with a yellowing 1963 proposal before the Federal Communications Commission. The proposition: to build a microwave voice communications link between Chicago and St. Louis.

McGowan had a new dream: to form such a network nationwide. The fact that the government hadn't sanctioned competition in the long-distance market didn't stop him. Says he: "AT&T had never expressly been given a monopoly in this market. Everyone just thought they had."

In 1969 the FCC approved the Chicago-to-St. Louis link of the MCI network. Meantime, McGowan hit the road in search of capital. Says he: "I went to bankers and venture capitalists. I even hit my brother up for $15,000." He was a fund raiser extraordinaire. Within four years of acquiring MCI, he'd earn more than $100 million. He'd also opened the maiden link of his network and, most important, had got the FCC to endorse the concept of nationwide long-distance phone competition. McGowan expanded MCA as fast as it could. It turned its first profit—$345,000—in 1977.

All this came in the face of tough competition from AT&T. It fought MCI in the marketplace, before the FCC, in Congress and the courts. "Why do you think I moved the company to Washington, D.C., half a block from the Federal Communications Commission?" he asks with a knowing smile.

AT&T's battle with MCI has proved expensive for both sides but may have been more costly for Ma Bell. In June 1980, a federal jury in Chicago ruled Ma Bell guilty of antitrust violations and ordered her to pay MCI $1.8 billion in damages—the largest antitrust judgment awarded to a company in U.S. history.

Meantime, McGowan keeps to the 70-plus-hour workweeks that have marked his career. A lifelong bachelor, he devotes almost all of his time to MCI. His principal diversion: supervising the renovation of three townhouses he owns overlooking the Potomac in Georgetown, one of which he plans eventually to make his home.

THE EXPRESS MAN

When Fred Smith was an undergraduate at Yale, he wrote a paper outlining an idea he had for revolutionizing the package delivery industry. He got a "C" grade for the paper. Today, ten years later, Fred's company, Federal Express, will have revenues of almost one billion dollars, doing exactly what he suggested doing in that original paper.

Much has happened in that intervening ten years. After graduating from Yale, Fred spent five years in Vietnam flying helicopters and other aircraft. Flying had always fascinated him ever since he learned to fly at age 15. While serving in Vietnam, he thought about his idea constantly, and it became an obsession with him after he left the service.

Fred was not to be a "rags to riches" entrepreneur since he inherited four million dollars—a lot of money by anyone's standards, but not enough to put together a nationwide organization involving sixty jet planes, hundreds of trucks, a huge distribution center in Memphis, Tennessee, and offices in every major city in the country. He brought together a group of young, eager, amibitious "go-for-broke" entrepreneurs—you had to be almost crazy to join this company in its early stages. But they hung in; they overcame the problems, and they won, against tremendous odds and against all the doubts and skepticism of everyone who said "it just isn't possible."

Fred could see that the computer was going to revolutionize business in America, and computers were dependent upon the fast delivery of vast amounts of data—information that had time value, that must be delivered where and when it was needed—now! Up until then, packages were delivered on a "best efforts, fastest possible" basis. You might get overnight service if the airlines had an ideal schedule, but there were no guarantees, and no one was willing to say that your package would positively, absolutely be delivered overnight.

So what was Fred's "better idea?" To fly all the packages to one central location in the country, resort them for their ultimate destinations, put them back on the planes and fly them out immediately, with a turn-around time of only four hours. And since he lived in Memphis, that was the city he chose as the hub.

The immediate need was for big money. And how do you convince a group of conservative, skeptical bankers that the fastest way to send a package from Detroit to Chicago was by way of Memphis? Another lesson that Fred learned was that when you borrow money, borrow lots of it. If you borrow only a little and need more, you have an unhappy creditor to deal with. If you borrow a lot, and things get tough, you've got a partner. Partners will bend over backwards to assist you.

And things did get tough. Before they made a penny of profit, the company lost twenty-nine million dollars. But they turned the corner, and as acceptance by the business community increased, sales and profits showed a steady climb. The company earned 1.24 per share in 1979, 2.06 in 1980, 2.89 in 1981, 3.70 in 1982 and will probably earn more than 4.00 in 1983. Since 1971 the stock price has ranged from a low of $6 per share to a high of $88½, which means the market is putting a value on the company of more than two billion dollars. Fred and the early entrepreneurs who joined him have reached total financial freedom.

146

Here is just one more example of how one man with a good, new idea, who can "see a need and fill it", working with the freedom and opportunity offered by the American free enterprise system, can create new wealth, provide a needed service to the public and make himself wealthy in the process.

THE OIL-WELL WILD-CATTER

Bill Brosseau is a man who enjoys flaunting his success—tooling around Dallas in his Cadillac limousine with his driver-chef, Johnny Christopher, or resting his snakeskin boots on his dazzling glass-and-brass dining room table after a hard day buying oil wells.

And success wears well on Brosseau (pronounced *Brew*-so). There are the $500 Southwick suits and $100 Turnbull & Asser shirts he wears to meetings with his wealthy clients, and the Sasson jeans and diamond-studded Corum watch he affects on expeditions to the oilfields. On someone else, all this might say rhinestone cowboy. But Brosseau, with his athletic six-foot, seven-inch frame, casts the image of a rakish Texas oilman.

As the owner of interests in 100 wells, Brosseau has come far fast. At 35, he has a personal worth of over $15 million and a $2.5 million annual income. When he was growing up in Junction City, Kans. and San Antonio, his family never had enough to make life comfortable. His father was an itinerant salesman. To the adolescent Bill Brosseau, the epitome of affluence was a friend's father, a local dentist. "He always seemed to have money," Brosseau recalls.

He went through the University of Texas on a basketball scholarship and on to Baylor University's dental school in Dallas. He became a dentist and married a woman who'd lived next door. Soon he became despondent. "I saw a psychiatrist," Brosseau recalls. "He told me that my only problems were that I hated my profession and my wife."

In 1975, Bill uncumbered himself of both. He became a stockbroker: "But you know what? I felt like a betting clerk. I just placed orders. I didn't feel I was adding much to the transactions."

Soon after Brosseau joined a brokerage firm, two acquaintances asked him to help line up investors for oil-drilling ventures in south and west Texas. Bringing in outside investors isn't unusual in the oil business. Drilling wells is expensive, and stockbrokers know many investors who can put up the funds for a syndicate.

"From day one," Brosseau says, "I felt this was the business for me. I understood the risk-reward ratio and I could see how you structure a deal." With beginner's luck, both of his initial deals were successful, producing oil and natural gas. In the better of the two, he'd managed to raise $100,000 from investors; he got in return a share of the well himself. Within a year, Brosseau's share was pumping $20,000 a *month* into his pocket—and that well is still pumping out the profits.

While luck dealt him a good opening hand, Brosseau concedes that he owes much of his subsequent fortune to the tutelage of M.B. Rudman, 71, whose acumen, gathered over 50 years in the oil business, has brought him more than $250 million. They met in 1978, just around the time that Brosseau said good-bye to stockbroking to be a full-time oilman, and Rudman took him on as a protege. Says Brosseau: "Duke Rudman put me five years ahead of where I'd have been on my own. He steered me toward the better-producing areas."

Using Rudman's wisdom, Brosseau evaluates promising

places to drill oil wells. Then he arranges acquisitions. Finally, he recruits investors who will put up the money. But through his one-man company, Argos Resources Inc., Brosseau also has to spend a good portion of his 60-hour workweek managing details involving the 100 wells in which he has an interest.

On his frequent trips to New York City and Chicago in search of cash, Brosseau is aided by his smooth manner and by the contacts he made as a broker. His 50 to 60 clients include tax attorneys, money managers and partners in large brokerage firms. In all, he has coaxed $30 million from his clients and invested $3 million of his own.

A few of his investors have struck it rich, but others have lost everything. "Some have dropped as much as $100,000," Brosseau says. "Usually when they lose that much they don't come back, although that's foolish. I'm persistent, that's why I'm good. I could hit 10 dry holes in a row and it wouldn't faze me."

Brosseau knows a series of setbacks only mean that big success is right around the next corner.

A MAN OF PROPERTY

Albert Lowry is the author of the all-time best selling real estate investment book, "How You Can Become Financially Independent Investing in Real Estate." His guide to investing in real estate has earned its author more than one million dollars. But Lowry doesn't need the money, and he has put the royalties into various trusts for his five children. His pleasure in doing so reaches past his success and back to his own unhappy childhood. Because his mother abused him, he was placed in a Winnipeg orphanage, where he spent much of his youth.

As a young man he worked at various jobs—from butcher's assistant to professional roller skater. When he met his future wife Darlene in 1961, he was 33, she was 19 and Lowry was drifting toward failure. But she was a stabilizing force, who moved him to extend himself. Within two years, Lowry and his bride left for the U.S. When they settled in the San Francisco Bay area, he had trouble finding a job. One day he spotted a newspaper ad with the appealing promise: MAKE BIG MONEY SELLING REAL ESTATE IN YOUR SPARE TIME. "I sure had plenty of that," he recalls. Several months passed before Lowry actually sold anything. But once he got going, he never stopped.

In mid-1964 he bought a small apartment house in Oakland. The place cost $52,000 but all Lowry put down was his $1,560 commission as the real estate agent on the sale. The deal epitomized his investment philosophy: keep down payments low and borrowing high. Over the next half-dozen years he bought single-mindedly and steadily. "We struggled for years," Darlene Lowry says. "We always put up everything we had so we could buy as much as possible." The tech-

151

nique worked. Lowry reckons that by 1971 their net worth exceeded $1 million.

By 1973, Lowry became bored with investing full time. So he cut down on his work and concentrated on composing a formal course in real estate investing. At first it floundered. Lowry lost $300,000 when he offered seminars nationally in 1975. But the endeavor ultimately caught on, and 100,000 people have gone through his classes. The bestseller: a weekend seminar for $445.

Today, the Lowrys own land in six states, office buildings and apartments in California and Nevada and a small parcel in Pittsburgh. They also own a 40-acre, $5 million mountaintop in Lake Tahoe, where they plan eventually to build a permanent home. Now they live in a relatively modest house nearby with their children—four boys and one girl ranging in age from five to 15. But they are building a $1.5 million extravaganza with decor that includes carpeting by Halston and copper walls in some bathrooms, silk in other.

Not bad for a fellow who left school in the eighth grade. Yet his lack of formal education left Lowry with a sense of insecurity. So he spent 1974 to 1976—between writing and lecturing—getting a Ph.D. in business administration from California Western University. Now Lowry relishes hearing himself called "Doctor," as he often does when he's out giving lectures. As with many entrepreneurs without much formal education, he desires status as well as money.

Lowry travels a lot these days, pushing one or another of his businesses. A few years ago he vowed he'd be able to retire before he was 50. That has given way to a new realization: "Hell, I'd die 10 days after I did." Lowery could retire today without any money worries, but he won't. His work is his life.

THE DOCTOR HUNTER

Though medical schools are graduating doctors so fast that many urban areas have become coagulated with physicians, there are still about 140 U.S. counties that have no doctors whatsoever. That's where Judith Berger, 37, comes in. Her Miami-based recruiting firm, M.D. Resources, tracks down physicians for jobs in smaller cities and rural communities as public health officers or in general practice. "Many doctors don't want to work those big-city schedules of 70 hours a week," Berger says. "They are willing to take a cutback in dollars in return for an improved quality of life."

Berger's own lifestyle has improved dramatically since her hectic childhood in West Hartford, Conn. While growing up, she was the subject of a prolonged custody between her biological mother and her adoptive parents, who ultimately won the case. The ordeal has made their relationship with their daughter especially close. Despite the turmoil, Berger went on to graduate from Franklin Pierce College in Rindge, N.H. at 19, majoring in "what everybody else did"—sociology and psychology—before finding work in a personnel agency recruiting secretaries.

After leaving her job to marry and have a son—she is now divorced—Berger took a job with a large Manhattan head-hunting firm that asked her to evaluate whether a health-care search business would succeed. She concluded it would and launched a doctor-hunting department. As revenues grew, so did the idea of going into business for herself. In 1979 the chance came to help start a medical recruiting firm in Miami. Her parents were already living there, so she was happy to move south. The new enterprise, however, quickly fell into hard times: one of her partners never put all the cash he'd promised into the business. Recalls Berger: "Our bills weren't being paid, our checks were bouncing, and I knew I had to get out."

She talked her parents and a couple of friends into lending her $40,000 to set up her own firm. Working out of a dimly lit cubbyhole that once served as a dentist's office, she bombarded hospitals and group medical practices with 5,000 letters letting them know she was in business. Now she has 15 employees searching through a computer bank of some 58,000 physicians for 48 clients. A search typically takes four months and costs the client $17,000 to $20,000. Last year M.D. Resources had reveneus of $1 million from recruiting 50 doctors for positions as diverse as hospital chief of staff and pediatric endocrinologist.

Meanwhile, Berger, whose $75,000 salary and $2.5 million net worth would be fit for any physician, has only begun to appreciate the financial rewards of her venture. "I never thought I'd be able to pay all my bills at one time and still have money left over in my checking account," she says. "But the best part of making money was being able to help send my parents on a trip to Israel last year."

THE CANDLEMAKER

Her friends, banker, even her dad pronounced her project hopeless. Cheerfully unfazed, Joyce Lund, 42, took the idea generated in the kitchen of her suburban Seattle home and turned it, by means of grit and womanpower, into a $5 million-a-year business. Now Lund's Lites is one of the biggest makers of decorative candles in the U.S. Among its inventive products: Baby Boo Bears—a pair of matching pink and blue bear candles for nurseries.

It all began in the fall of 1971 when Lund needed some extra cash to buy Christmas presents for her six children. She had made candles before but had always given them away as gifts. Then a friend who dropped by one morning offered a suggestion: Why not sell some of her homemade candles?

So, melting wax on her kitchen stove, Lund started turning out candles like, well, hotcakes. She set up a display shelf in her living room and spread the word. Recalls Lund: "People started coming to the house in droves. They were buying candles as fast as I could make them."

Lund, and husband Howard, an air traffic controller, took to turning out candles through the night, napping in alternating two-hour shifts. Lund called friends and relatives and asked them to work for her. Some helped make candles; others sold them, holding Tupperware-style parties in other people's homes. "Everyone says you're not supposed to hire friends or relatives or untrained housewives," she says, "but I did it from the begining and still do."

155

In early 1973, she moved the business from her home to a small warehouse. Recalls Lund: "The owners demanded that we sign a month-to-month lease. They thought we were a bunch of kooky, bored housewives who wouldn't last a year." Bankers evidently thought so too. When Lund sought her first loan, for a mere $500, her husband had to cosign. Not to be dismayed, she held fast to her dream.

In 1978, Lund's Lites moved into the 20,000-square-foot factory where Lund and her employees recently celebrated her being named Pacific Northwest Woman Entrepreneur of the Year. Today the company sells candles in 30 states. Lund won't reveal her net worth but avers: "I thought millionaires were supposed to have chauffeurs and maids. I don't."

Joyce Lund may not have chaufferurs and maids (but she could afford to), what she does have is the satisfaction of knowing that she is magic, she can make it happen!

THE MALPRACTICE MAN

In Houston, where big money usually means oil, gas or real estate, Richard Cross, 41, is a refreshing change. He earned his more than $5 million personal fortune in insurance. As the founder and chief executive of the Insurance Corp. of America, Cross heads a $30 million-a-year firm that sells malpractice coverage to doctors and lawyers.

What truly makes Cross a rebel is neither his locale nor his product. It's his uncanny timing and sheer business guts. Crossbfounded ICA in 1975, a year in which other, more established malpractice insurers—such as the Travelers Corp.—were fleeing the market. Reason for the panic: a spate of highly publicized, multimillion-dollar malpractice judgments against doctors in a few states, notably New York. When the big companies pulled out, Cross moved in.

"At the time," recalls the lean, homespun Cross, who grew up as the only child of an Oklahoma farmer and oilfield laborer, "the big boys in the insurance business were scared out of their minds. They saw every Tom, Dick and Harry lining up to sue. All they wanted to do was get the hell out of town. That's when I thought there might be a place for me."

If there *was* a place for him, he was well positioned to find it. He was an accountant and a lawyer with some experience in medical malpractice cases. He also was a bondsman, and as such had a license to write insurance policies. "I'd never written a malpractice policy," says he, "but I knew enough about insurance to realize that the big buys had to be doing something wrong." What Cross saw was that the major carriers were overreacting by either pricing themselves out of the market or settling cases too easily.

So Cross jumped into the malpractice business. "People told me I ought to have my head examined," he recalls. "It was funny, though. I thought *they shoulM have their* heads examined. I'd done my homework, and I knew that if I charged a reasonable rate and fought the cases where my clients were right, I'd do okay." He also decided to stay out of states where malpractice suits were common.

In its first year, Cross' ICA took in about $1 million in malpractice premiums. Now, selling through independent agents in 20 states and the District of Columbia, ICA expects to take in about $1 million a week in revenues in 1983.

Cross lives well but not extravagantly in Houston's River Oaks section. "The trappings don't mean a damn thing," says the divorced father of one whose 11-year-old son lives with his mother in Tucson. "My satisfaction is having a company that I built and love. It's also in knowing that those people were wrong when they told me I was out of my mind."

THE LIQUIDATOR

His name sends fear through the companies whose stock he owns. Irwin L. Jacobs—a.k.a. "Irv the Liquidator"—is the brash Minneapolis millionaire known best for buying ailing companies and putting them out of their misery by selling their assets and usually turning a tidy profit for himself. For more than 20 years, Jacobs, 44, has been buying what no one else wants.

At 18, Jacobs, ready to spend the $4,000 or so he'd made working in his father's burlap-bag manufacturing business, attended a U.S. Customs auction. One sale was a shipment of Italian skis that had been confiscated for tariff violations. Jacobs paid $13 a pair for several hundred pairs. Says he: "I took the skis out on the street and people started coming up to me and asking how much I wanted for them. I said $39 a pair. I sold some on the spot and the rest within a few weeks. I made $10,000 on the deal." The die was cast.

It was the first of many profitable deals for Jacobs. While still working in the family business, he would go to retailers, buy damaged goods or unsold inventories and resell at a profit. In 1975, at 33, he started buying companies. His first purchase: a failing local outfit called Grain Belt Breweries. After 10 months of trying to get the staggering beermaker back on its feet, Jacobs sold off most of its assets at a profit of $4 million.

Today his bargain hunter's sights are set on even bigger game. Jacobs and a group of other investors have made a tender offer in an effort to gain control of Pabst Brewing Co. Says he: "I think I can do a better job of running it than the present directors." The present Pabst directors fear that Irv the Liquidator might pour Pabst down the drain.

159

Jacobs, who lives with his wife and five children in the 30-room house that was the set for the 1972 movie *The Heartbreak Kid*, says he wants to correct two misconceptions. "First," says he, "I'm not worth anywhere near the $50 million that I've heard quoted. Second, I *did* go to college—for three days, and then I went back into business.

Jacobs may be worth only half of the fifty million some say he has, but that still isn't bad for a guy who likes to buy and sell things.

THE ADVERTISING ADVOCATE

Barbara Gardner Proctor was born illegitimate in the mountains of North Carolina. Now she owns a Chicago advertising agency that had billings of $12.8 million last year and counts among its clients Kraft, Sears and Jewel Food Stores. There have been plenty of bumps along the way, but Proctor has succeeded because she has a lot of determination and an absolute sense of what she wants to accomplish. She recalls that her grandmother used to say of her: "She's not cute, but she's right smart." Smart! That's an understatement!!

Proctor, 50, was raised by that grandmother in dirt-poor Black Mountain, N.C., where she had neither running water nor electricity. She did manage to get a college education at Talladega College in Alabama, but then spent years drifting from job to job. In 1956 a love of jazz and a flair for writing brought her to Vee-Jay Records in Chicago. She was hired to write descriptive comments on album covers; within a year she was doing jazz commentary for Downbeat magazine.

In 1960, she married Carl Proctor, Sarah Vaughan's road manager. The union lasted just two years, but it produced a son, Morgan, 19. (Already a part of his mother's business for several years, Morgan hopes eventually to run the agency.) After her divorce, Proctor left the record industry so she wouldn't keep running into Carl. Her writing skill got her a job as a copywriter for a Chicago ad agency. She worked for three different agencies in five years, ultimately earning $40,000 a year. "I was a hot property," she says.

She was certain that the time was right for an ad agency addressing black consumers and that her talents were bankable.

161

So she applied for a loan guaranteed by the Small Business Administration. Being in a service industry and having no collateral, she normally would have had little chance. But she persuaded a loan officer to ask the heads of three Chicago agencies what salary they would pay her. The answers came back: $65,000, $80,000 and $110,000. With her unshakable self-assurance, Proctor got an $80,000 loan.

When she launched her agency in 1970, she named it Proctor & Gardner Advertising. "That way, it sounds like there's a man named Gardner behind me," she explains, "and that gives people a more secure feeling when they deal with me." An early client was Jewel Foods, the large mid-western supermarket chain. Harry Segal, its advertising vice president, explains why Jewel chose Proctor: "When we decided to stay in the black neighborhoods of Chicago, we wanted to communicate our commitment to the community. Barbara Proctor's agency was the only one we could trust to have the skill and sensitivity to do the job right."

Through the years, Proctor has smoothly handled tough assignments, such as the introduction of generic foods, Segal says. "At first blacks thought it was just cheap junk being thrown at them. But after Proctor's campaign, generics were accepted and have been big sellers ever since." Her newspaper, radio and TV ads typified her style—clear, direct messages that got right down to value for your money.

Recently, Proctor was elected to the board of Illinois Bell Telephone Co. Says William Springer, the company's chief financial officer: "Barbara crackles with a sense of the market. She understands the black community, and that's something the phone company needs.

Proctor is secretive about her wealth. She has often been described as a "self-made millionaire." Says she with a laugh: "I won't disclaim any of that, but I won't be any more specific."

Looking forward to composing more than ads, Proctor has great expectations: she plans to write a book that will reassure women about their worth. "I'd like to call it *Bury Me in a Size 6*," says Proctor, who wears a size 12. "Women usually harbor fears of not gaining approval. I'd like to address those fears."

THE EMPLOYMENT FINDER

If now is a hard time to start a business, so too was April 1974. But it was good enough for Ruth Clark. Despite a recession and a prime rate rising toward a then inconceivable 11%, Clark took $3,900 of her savings and started Clark Unlimited Personnel. Says she: "I'm the type who turns every negative into a positive."

The clients of Clark's Manhattan firm are corporations that need workers mainly to fill temporary clerical and secretarial positions. Annual revenues top $2 million. Perhaps equally gratifying to Clark, 40: "We keep 1,500 to 2,000 people a year employed." About 70% of them are black. Says she: "I provide good service for everyone, but I'm very happy that I've done well for my own people."

Clark launched her own business only after learning the ropes working for several years in a similar New York City placement firm. The first few months were decidedly hand to mouth. When she couldn't get a bank loan, Clark turned to factoring houses, which lend to high-risk businesses on the basis of the money that is owed to them by customers. Such lenders command premium interest rates—in Clark's case, 21% on the $12,000 she borrowed.

She zeroed in on leading New York City companies that were eager to do business with minority-owned firms. Among her clients today are Chase Manhattan Bank, Bankers Trust, Irving Trust and the three major broadcasting networks. Says she: "I never aim for the middle. I go straight for the top." Born and raised in Harlem, Clark, a divorced woman, now lives in a $1 million co-op in the same Sutton Place building as designer Calvin Klein.

THE BOOKKEEPER
WHO BECAME AN ENTREPRENEUR

At 37, Billye Ericksen was a divorced mother of three, supporting her family with a series of dead-end jobs as a clerk/typist at Lockheed, Philco and RCA. Now she's 50, married again—calling herself Ericksen-Desaigoudar—and owns an $8 million-a-year electronic-parts wholesaling company that pays her a salary of $150,000. It's hard to say which quality helped her more: chutzpah or brains. Probably a combination of the two!

With only a high school education and some night courses in accounting, she eventually talked her way into a bookkeeper's job at a small high-tech company in Mountain View, CA. Before long she was the controller, creating better financial controls and suggesting ways to improve other company operations. But when she bluntly told a board meeting that her $21,800 salary didn't reflect the value of her contributions, she was out on her ear.

Then in 1977 she found employment as the controller of a little electronic-parts distributor with a staff of 30 in Sunnyvale, CA. It was the perfect vehicle for her. "I drew up the company's first long-range sales plan," she says proudly. She also lost no time pointing out to the president that his friend, the company's lawyer, was earning more in fees than he was making as chief executive. Four months later the law firm was replaced.

In 1981 her boss, who had other business interests, asked Ericksen, by then chief financial officer, to take the company off his hands. She was able to buy him and the other shareholders out for $1 million, which she borrowed from a

165

bank. By 1984, when she finishes paying off the loan, she'll control the company.

Capacitor Sales, its name changed by its new owner to Capsco Sales, snoozes no more. Since Ericksen took charge in 1981, the company has become a major distributor for Panasonic, Unitrode, Sangamo and Murata/Erie products. This year she reckons sales will be up 25%. All in all, Capsco does twice the business today that it did in the years before Ericksen woke it up.

THE SILVER LINING

As president and chief executive of Towle Manufacturing Co., a venerable maker of sterling silverware, Leonard Florence is a powerhouse is the business. Florence, 49, the sixth of eight children of a Russian-Jewish immigrant milkman in Chelsea, Mass., a decaying seaport suburb of Boston, is not surprised by his rise. But Yankee silversmiths look on him as an outsider.

At Boston University, Florence won a Dewey Stone scholarship. After graduation, he was offered a job by Stone, a Boston industrialist. If Florence could rescue Raimond Silver, a failing giftware company that Stone owned, he would get a half-interest in the firm.

By discarding slow selling lines and manufacturing products for well-known firms, Florence turned Raimond into a solid profit maker. When Stone sold Raimond in 1968, half of the $2.1 million price went to Florence. That enabled him to start his own company, Leonard Silver Manufacturing, which produces silver-plated trays, bowls and pitchers. It had become a $39 million company by the time he merged it with Towle in 1978. An old-line firm, Towle has a sparkling credit rating, which has helped Florence raise the cash to buy companies that turn out glassware, stainless-steel flatware and china. Sales last year were $143 million.

Florence is worth $20 million to $25 million ("Not bad for a boy from Chelsea—huh") and drives a Rolls-Royce Silver Shadow II. But the car spends scant time in the driveway of his 16-room house in Brookline, Mass. Florence rarely sees his wife and three children. "When you work this hard," he says, "you miss things—like your children growing up."

SPEAKING FOR PROFITS

Soon after coming to America (High Point, NC) in 1966, a local church asked the college freshman to speak to its congregation about life in the Middle East. Recalls Qubein (pronounced Kuh-*bane*), who then could utter only a few English phrases: "I stumbled, told jokes nobody laughed at, spoke too fast, had no organization and bored everyone to death." But by practicing what he preaches to his current audiences—"Don't stick your foot in a door to keep it from slamming; use your head so you can keep talking"—Qubein, now 36, has become a much-in-demand, motivational speaker, charging $2,500 for a 45-minute talk, and the proprietor of two businesses in High Point: Creative Services and Nido Qubein & Associates, with combined revenues of nearly $1 million, one-third of which Quebein gets to keep.

The die for Qubein's career was set while he was attending the University of North Carolina business school. He noticed that many of the students were unable to communicate effectively and for that reason appeared to lack leadership qualities. No sooner had he received his M.B.A.; in 1972 than he immediately spent $500 promoting a newsletter and tape cassettes in which he talked about how to become a leader.

In 1979, Qubein got a great insight. Says he: "I used to tell my audiences, 'You can climb the highest mountian,' but then I realized that I had to describe *how* to climb the mountain to be genuinely effective." So he began creating "action plans" for such corporate clients as Dole Processed Foods and INA Bearing Co.

In a typical weeklong seminar, for example, Qubein explains his four basic steps for successful selling: discovering and evaluating prospective customers, skillfully presenting the product, preparing for any possible objections the customer might have and, finally, asking for an order. Qubein now has 18 clients paying between $25,000 and $80,000 a year for his action plans, depending on how often he visits the company.

There are hundreds of great motivation speakers, but Qubein puts on a memorable show, bouncing from easel to blackboard, gliding from one anecdote to another in a liquid Lebanese accent. Nearly 70% of his business last year came from companies that had hired him before. "They want me back because I didn't just tell their employees that they could do better," he said, "I *showed* them how."

THE REAL ESTATE DEVELOPER

Real estate is still the surest road to riches—particularly for someone persistent enough to sense what type of project will prosper and convincing enough to sell his ideas to financial backers and prospective buyers and tenants. It also helps to be located in a booming area, notably the golden state of California. Just ask Cal Rossi. At 45 he is already worth $18 million. Now the man who created San Francisco's top luxury hotel, Stanford Court, and developed many other projects around California, is taking on ever-grander ones.

Even as a teenager, Anthony Cal Rossi Jr. showed the far-sighted vision that developers need to succeed. Working in the San Joaquin Valley fig orchards owned by his father, a prosperous rancher with a spread near Fresno, Rossi could see the possibility of opening up some of the family farmland. He persuaded his parents to let him put together a shopping center and apartment complex on 25 acres. Through high school and college he worked to secure necessary permits, hire an architect, find tenants, raise the money and finally build the project. That development, which Rossi still owns, has been a steady money-maker for him.

From 1950 to 1968, he built and managed restaurants, put up single-family homes in several northern California towns, developed a second-home subdivision in the Sierra Nevada east of Fresno and even acted as a restaurant consultant. One of his clients was the Mark Hopkins Hotel in San Francisco.

In 1961, Rossi bought Stanford Court, a run-down apartment building on Nob Hill. Borrowing $11.3 million from Connecticut General Insurance Co. and $5 million from

170

United Airlines, he demolished the apartments and built a 402-room luxury hotel. The five-star Stanford Court now has both the highest room rates, an average of $130 a night, and the highest occupancy, 85% to 90% in the city.

Stanford Court made Rossi's reputation, but he sold his interest in it in 1972 because he couldn't agree with his two partners on the management of the hotel. Though he made a $2 million profit on the deal, the hotel has recently been earning $6 million a year, and Rossi laments, "I wish I'd never sold."

Since then he has bought and transformed a second San Francisco hotel, the 140-room Pacific Plaza. Its $2.5 million lobby has Italian-marble floors and walls, hand-blown Venetian-glass chandeliers, antiques and old tapestries. Rossi is building even bigger projects—a $90 million, 750-family second home and retirement community east of San Diego; a 300-room, $38 million oceanfront hotel on the Monterey peninsula; and a $25 million renovation of the historic Jergins Trust office building in Long Beach. In each case, Rossi's role is slightly different. While he owns the retirement project outright, he is part owner and managing partner of the other two.

Rossi and Cecilia, his wife of 23 years, and their three teenage children live in a San Francisco mansion, one of the five homes they own around the state. Their favorite is a six-bedroom house that was built on a barge, then floated up the bay to an 850-acre island they own in the Sacramento River delta, where it is moored. The family spends summer weekends at the island; during duck hunting season, Cal Rossi brings along friends and associates. A man who likes nothing better than to be closest to the fire, Rossi always does the cooking.

171

ATTORNEY TO THE MASSES

With his "honest" looks and manner, Joel Hyatt seems right at home starring as a pitchman in TV commercials. But he's no ordinary announcer hawking soap, beer or cars. He's both the mouthpiece and senior partner of Hyatt Legal Services, dispenser of inexpensive wills ($45), divorces ($250) and bankruptcy petitions ($350). So convincing a salesman is Hyatt that in 1980 he talked H&R Block, the tax preparers, into a mutual assistance pact for which Block paid $2 million in cash to Joel Hyatt and a partner—with more to come.

Hyatt, 34, brings elegant credentials to his mostly storefront offices. A Clevelander, he began his career more auspiciously than most lawyers at the prestigious firm of Paul Weiss Rifkind in New York City. In 1976, he managed the U.S. Senate election campaign of Howard Metzenbaum, the Ohio Democrat. Metzenbaum won the seat and Hyatt won the hand of his daughter Susan. After than, corporate law seemed unfulfilling. "Lawyers are supposed to serve the public," says Hyatt. "I could see a vast public—maybe 70% of the American people—going unserved because they couldn't afford a lawyer."

When the Supreme Court opened the door for lawyers to advertise, Hyatt saw at once that he could slash the price of legal services by mass-marketing them. No other attorney saturated his market with ads as heavily as Hyatt did in Cleveland. In two years he was running 10 offices.

H&R Block made their fortune in much the same way years before with tax advice. And when Hyatt heard that Block wanted to make its business less seasonal, he wisely sensed a chance at symbiosis. Strictures against legal-fee splitting kept Block from acquiring the firm. Instead, in a unique deal, a Block subsidiary was set up that sells nonlegal services to Hyatt and he financed its expansion to 65 locations in nine states. Joel Hyatt gets a salary of about $100,000 per year, but, more important, he also collected over 10% of the subsidiary's stock. He can sell it back to Block after several years at a price that's said to be "generous."

STAY-AT-HOME SUCCESS

When Paul Stanislaw looks into his bathroom mirror every morning, he gets motivated. Not by his determined, earnest face but by a plethora of platitudes pasted on the glass: GO THAT EXTRA MILE...DON'T EVER QUIT, DON'T EVER RETREAT...YOU'LL BE NO. 1. Stanislaw, 38, concedes that the sayings may be hokey. But they have helped make him the No. 3 salesperson in the country for Investors Diversified Services (IDS), which sells mutual funds, life insurance, limited partnerships and other financial products and services nationwide. Last year, Stanislaw's sales totaled $8.4 million and he earned $180,000 in commissions. What is most remarkable is that he has done it without leaving his home town, Warren, Ohio (pop. 56,600), in an area with one of the nation's highest unemployment rates—19.7%.

Stanislaw uses vast energy and unyeilding persistence and community contacts to woo his 800 clients, mostly middle-aged steel and automotive workers. "I understand the people here," he explains. "A lot of my customers are friends of my parents. I know what they have to go through and I tell them that their money should work for them." Based on his clients' financial goals and available capital, Stanislaw develops a long-term strategy and recommends—but never hard sells—IDS components to make the plan work.

His drive for total success originated from his keen desire to break away from the factory life of Warren. His father, now retired, was a steelworker for 37 years. Stanislaw himself had a production-line job at a local General Motors plant after graduating from high school in 1965. But he studied for his bachelor's degree at night and eventually became a

$26,000 industrial engineer at GM. Soon he was frustrated by the confines of corporate life. "I could imagine retiring 35 years later without ever having been challenged," he says. So when a local high school coach turned IDS salesman asked him to join the team in 1979, Stanislaw jumped. He spent that first year learning his new trade. Nevertheless, he managed to sell $2 million worth of IDS products, earning $32,000. In 1980 he was named Rookie of the Year by IDS and more than doubled his salary. This year he hopes to earn $250,000.

Stanislaw takes his own investment advice. He has invested $150,000 in IDS oil and gas and real estate partnerships, mutual funds and annuities. He also owns three rental apartments worth $250,000 and recently renovated a Victorian house. He is planning to buy a commercial building in downtown Warren to use for IDS offices. Other salesmen of the company will rent space from him. Most IDS representatives work out of their homes, but Stanislaw feels it is important to have a permanent, visible office. "People in the community will see the building and know that IDS is in the area to stay," he asserts. Stanislaw is there to stay too. He is willing to go that extra mile!

FROM POLICEMAN PETROL PROFITEERING

A job selling fuel ignited Larry Wardlaw's ambition to build his own company. The son of a housemaid, Wardlaw says: "I knew that I wanted to be in a better financial situation than my mother." After working his way through the University of New Haven as a part-time office administrator at the National Cash Register Corp., Wardlaw, now 37, joined the firm full time as a salesman. Later, disenchanted with sales, he left to walk a beat as a patrolman in New Haven's tough inner city for six months. "Although it was one of the worst jobs I had," Wardlaw recalls, "it gave me insight into people—a great asset in business."

Realizing the big danger and low income of police work, Wardlaw went back to sales. In 1973, he set up a marketing program for a small New Haven fuel-distributing firm. He helped fan sales from $5 million to $25 million in five years. But the business was owned by a local family, and he had no chance of running it. So, armed with $10,000 in savings and a $220,000 Small Business Administration loan, which he got because he had five years of experience in the field, he started his own fuel-distribution company, Wardoco. It buys petroleum products from suppliers and transports them in its fleet of seven trucks to customers.

Even though Wardoco's first two years coincided with the period when oil prices jumped over the moon, the company lost money because it didn't have enough major accounts. So Wardlaw dropped his residential customers in favor of bigger commercial clients, who buy in bulk. Hard selling and a varied product line that includes aviation fuels, lubricants and heating oil helped Wardlaw push revenues from $17 million in 1980 to $85 million last year, when profits hit $1 million. Wardoco is now the third largest minority-owned business in the U.S. Its customers include Yale University, Amtrak and the city of New Haven.

Wardlaw admits that he's very aggressive. "To get that kind of sales growth in such a short time you cannot be a low-key person," he says. Nor can you be a nine-to-fiver. "If I'm not in the office working, I'm at home at the dining room table working," he says ruefully. He earns $100,000 a year as president of Wardoco and lives with his wife and two children in a suburb of New Haven—a far cry but not many miles away from the ghetto where he was raised.

GAMES MAN

When Gary Gabrel, 33, of Stillwater, OK, decided six years ago to develop a board game called Pente, he made all the right moves. His is an unusual product for the high-tech 1980s: it doesn't require an electrical outlet to be played, and it doesn't pit the players against invaders from outer space. The game is a cross between checkers and tic-tac-toe. Players move different colored beads across a grid with the object of lining up five in a row—hence the name, Pente. The game's simple challenge and Gabrel's shrewd marketing strategy have transformed a pizza-parlor manager into a corporate chairman who earns about $75,000 a year and is worth more than $1 million.

Games have always fascinated Gabrel, especially those that required mental skills. Unsure how to apply his hobby to a career, he took a job managing the pizzeria in Stillwater, where he had worked part time while attending Oklahoma State. After hours, the restaurant became a club. The staff and close friends played cards, chess, backgammon and Monopoly till dawn. During one of these sessions, somebody introduced a derivative of the ancient Japanese game called Go. Fascinated, Gabrel decided to adapt it for Americans.

Browsing in his local library, he came upon a drawing of the Greek heroes Achilles and Ajax seated across a table playing a game that resembled go. This inspired the distinctive design of the board, which is edged with Greek figures and ornamentation. Since Pente is based on a game that has been around for centuries, Gabrel couldn't patent it. So he copyrighted the name and the board.

In 1977 he borrowed $20,000 to finance a run of 1,000 sets and began hawking them to Stillwater retailers. To stimulate demand, he left Pente sets at singles bars in Oklahoma City and Houston, and soon people were asking for the game in stores. After that, he was able to get independent national sales representatives to handle his product. Sales grew from 300 games in 1978 to 450,000 last year. Prices range from $15 for a travelers' version, which comes in a tube, to $100 for a deluxe wood model.

Gabrel has several new games on the drawing board, but his main goal is to advance Pente. This year he'll spend $150,000 promoting a world championship Pente tournament in Boston. Back in 1978, game manufacturers refused Gabrel's offer to market his product, but recently Selchow & Righter, manufacturers of Scrabble, indicated an interest in buying it. Gabrel's reply: "No-thanks." He is having too much fun and also making very good money.

HIGH-TECH PROFITS

John Duncan didn't want to leave the Rockies to practice his high-technology profession, so he brought his trade to the mountains. In 1967 he started Summit Engineering in a basement in Bozeman, Mont. He concentrated on an almost untapped market: small machine manufacturers in need of sophisticated electronics to speed up production. By 1981 the company had $16 million in sales. Recently Duncan, who has a net worth of $500,000, started a new Bozeman company: Tele-Tech, a manufacturer and designer of electronics products for use in communication and navigation systems.

Born and raised in Wyoming, Duncan, 51, worked his way through the University of Wyoming as a horse wrangler and corral boss. When he went to Montana State University for his Ph.D. in electrical engineering, he was taken with the city of Bozeman. But it had no major engineering firms. "I always intended to start a business, and if I wanted to live in Bozeman and be a design engineer, I had no choice," says Duncan. He started the business with just $80, but soon his designs helped Summit climb to the top of its field. Its best-known product: the Bandit, a programmable tool-control system that when connected to a drill, for instance, gives orders to reproduce the holes in a circuit board.

In 1974, in need of capital for his rapidly expanding enterprise, Duncan sold Summit to the Dana Corp., a conglomerate, for $1 million in stock and cash. He stayed on as president of Summit. Then, a year ago, Dana promoted him to manage six plants in its electronic-controls division. Duncan was clearly on his way up, but that would have meant relocating to Toledo. That didn't suit him at all, instead heleft Summit and Dana last April to start Tele-Tech. He raised $400,000 to buy back from Dana the product line of radio-frequency components that he had developed. "It's an ideal time to go into the radio and television transmission field," he asserts. "We are selling to small and large businesses in satellite TV and cable TV." By the end of 1982, having signed on such customers as Rockwell International and General Electric, Tele-Tech had turned a profit—further proof from Duncan that you can make it big in small places. And making big money in the environment he loves, is what the good life is all about for John Duncan.

MARKETING WIZARD

Jane Evans was cut from rare fabric. It is ironic that the apparel business, a field devoted to adorning the feminine form, can boast of few women who wear the pants. Those who have made it to the top have done so by designing their own fashion lines. Jane Evans made it by design too, but her talent is as a marketer and manager. At 40, she is head of the General Mills Fashion Group, which includes Izod Lacoste, Lark luggage, Ship 'n Shore sportswear, Monet costume jewelry and Foot-Joy shoes. Evans earns more than $200,000 a year and has a hefty perk package including stock options tied to corporate performance.

Long before graduating from Vanderbilt University in 1965, she was recruited by Genesco, where she became assistant buyer for I. Miller, its retail shoe division. Maxey Jarman, Genesco's late eccentric chairman, liked Evans' ideas and moxie and, five years later, at 25, made her I. Miller's president. (During those years she met and married George Sheer, a shoe importer; they have a nine-year-old son, Jonathan.) At 29, she was recruited by the American Can Co. to become president of Butterick Fashion Marketing, the pattern company. After three years she left to rejuvenate Fingerhut, a mail-order retailer based in Minneapolis.

Evans credits her corporate climbs to her enormous ability to deal with people and inherent grasp of consumer marketing. She seems to know just what to do to turn an ailing business around. At I. Miller, she changed the dowdy company so it would appeal to younger customers. At Butterick, she redirected the sagging Vogue pattern line to attract working women who wanted elegant styles but simplified pat-

182

terns.

Besides her other talents, Evans was tapped for the New York-based General Mills job because she is a team player. As she says: "I'm not a lone ranger." During the next year, Evans has her managerial work cut out for her. Responsible for five companies, she plans to strengthen her group's line of athletic wear, increase its accessories business through acquisitions and develop an entirely new clothing division for executive women.

SOFTWARE SUCCESS

How many times can you lose your job with a company before they beg you to come back as chairman? For John Imlay, 49, the answer was twice. In 1968, he joined an Atlanta firm called Management Science America as vice president for marketing. MSA produces standard-application software—the off-the-shelf programs that tell computers how to operate. No sooner had Imlay been hired than he was telling the president that MSA should dump its consulting business and slash overhead. The president's response: dumping Imlay instead. A new president rehired him a few months later, only to can him again when Imlay insisted the company needed to reform its free-spending ways. But by 1971, when MSA's debts greatly exceeded its assets, the company's two major creditors, $8 million in the hole, called Imlay back and told him to bring his scythe with him.

Now approximately ten years later, Imlay had transformed a company with a net loss of $7 million on $9 million in sales in 1970 to one with 1981 revenues of $73 million and earnings of $5.5 million. He draws an annual salary of $240,000 and owns 24.7% of the company, a holding worth about $67 million.

Imlay's first move was to reorganize the company under Chapter X bankruptcy proceedings. His second was even more jolting: in three grueling days he fired more than 700 employees, paring the staff to a skeletal 50. He then set to work developing a strong marketing and sales force. By 1981, MSA was able to go public, and Imlay figured he could afford to buy another Atlanta firm, Peachtree Software Inc., which produces software packages for IBM's personal computer.

Despite that wholesale firing, Imlay considers himself a master at motivating people. He calls everybody Tiger and led one of the big cats live into an employee meeting to emphasize the need for fearlessness and perserverance in reaching company goals. MSA now has 1,134 employees and is the country's largest independent supplier of application software. But Imlay has another objective: "I want to become a major corporation while retaining a personal touch."

PAT SWIFT

Once upon a time, it seemed that clothing designers created fashions only for dolls and the malnourished. But because manufacturers have broadened their collections to include chic styles for large women, models over five feet seven inches tall and weighing up to 200 pounds are in demand. That has created a thriving market for Pat Swift's Plus Model Management. Swift, 29, and a size 18, opened her modeling agency five years ago. Business was lean at first, but last year her stable of statuesque clothes-horses earned $750,000 in fees, and she expects billings to zoom past one million by 1985.

A 1976 graduate of the University of South Florida with a degree in criminal justice, Swift's move into modeling was serendipitous. While working as a detective in Bloomingdale's, she was approached by a representative of Act III, a women's sportswear company, to work as a large-size model. "I was so surprised," says the dimple-cheeked brunette. "I thought I was kind of unattractive." An ad in the New York Times featuring Swift spurred her to quit Bloomingdale's. "At first I made the rounds of modeling jobs myself anyway." she says. "And people were asking me if I knew any other large-size models." In May 1978 she started her own agency on $3,500 in savings and recruited her first dozen models through newspaper ads. Now she employs 50, including eight petite women—five feet five inches tall and 100 pounds soaking wet—and eight big men, six-footers weighing in at 230 to 290 pounds. All fit her three-Ps formula for success: a good personality, good proportions and a pretty or handsome face.

Swift's success flows in part from a desire to prove that unusually big people can be commercially successful. "I was the large one in a family of thin people. I know what it's like not to accept your appearance," she says. Because many of her models are unhappy with their size and want to lose weight, Swift gives a 12-week course in feeling good about yourself to new recruits. She has advanced her crusade as the co-author of *The Full-Figured Woman's Guide to Beauty—Great Looks* (Doubleday, $19.95), now in its second printing. Work consumes so much of Swift's life that she hasn't taken a vacation since the agency opened. But she does live it up on her $100,000 salary. Last year she bought a mink coat, a Salvador Dali lithograph and new furniture for her Park Avenue apartment.

THE TOOL PEDDLER

New Englander, Pierre de Beaumont was 50 years old when he and his wife Deland founded the Brookstone Co., a mail-order tool business, at their kitchen table. They began the company in western Massachusetts with $500 in 1965 and sold it to Quaker Oats in 1980 for $9 million worth of its stock—proving you're never too old to get rich.

De Beaumont, who had been a Ford dealer and later a manager with a papermill machinery company, created Brookstone on the premise that people need all sorts of tools they can't find in hardware stores. For instance, a jeweler's holding jig is perfect for clamping model-railroad parts together at the correct angle for soldering. "As far as we could tell, no one else was selling that sort of thing." de Beaumont says. "But we didn't know whether it was a hole in the market or a hole to fall into."

After reading everything he could get his hand on regarding mail-order, he sent away for obscure tools he might sell, he printed a folder offering 42 items and sent it to 3,000 hobbyists. Business built up slowly—to flood level. The de Beaumonts, with a little part-time help, found themselves working seven days a week, 12 hours a day. "We ran absolutely flat out at all times," recalls de Beaumont. "We couldn't even afford to get the flu."

In 1969, with Brookstone grossing $250,000 a year, de Beaumont let up enough to hire a manager and moved most of the company from his home near Pittsfield, Mass. to a plant in Peterborough, N.H. Annual sales now are $27 million. Some steady sellers: a miniature anvil and a thingamajig that removes nails from shingles. Brookstone offers 600 tools in its main catalogue, 5 million of which go out three times a year, and the company owns eight retail stores in the East. The founding father, now 65, has moved to a shorefront house north of Boston. He wanted to retire sooner, he says, but held on until he had a decent hedge against inflation. With his Quaker Oats shares, he's well hedged.

THE CONDO KING

When Robert Morris arrived in Sarasota from the University of Florida in Gainesville in 1970, he was 27 years old and had only $350 in his jeans. But he brought with him a brand-new architect's degree and an itch to build. On half a mile of Sarasota Bay waterfront and around a pelican-populated cove, he soon envisioned low-rise condominiums amid the mangrove, oak and hickory trees of the southwest Florida coast.

That was his goal. Now he had to raise the money—to begin with, $1.5 million to buy the land. He would first have to prove himself on a smaller project. As a graduate student, he had designed and built a 58-unit student-housing project. On the slender thread of that experience he mapped out a similar project in Tampa and, with bank loans hard to get, sought financing from insurance companies. After many rejections, he got the money from Connecticut Mutual Life.

Not until 1972, when the Tampa development was nearly completed, did Morris convince Connecticut Mutual to finance Pelican Cove in Sarasota. But that project established his reputation as an environmentally conscious developer— a rarity among Florida builders then. Rather than bulldoze Pelican Cove's 75 acres, he hired young men to clear the vegetation with machetes and chain saws, preserving most of the trees and pelican rookeries.

During the seven years it took to complete Pelican Cove, Morris put six other projects. Far more important, he built an impeccable credit rating. During the 1974-75 recession, when 60% of Florida's developers halted operations, Morris was able to keep building. Last year his company, the Ramar Group Inc., had profits of around $7.5 million. Its newest project, just begun, is the Plantation, near Venice, Fla., with 4,000 houses and condos, plus shopping, offices, a resort hotel and a country club. Morris is secretive about his net worth. Best guess is somewhere between $6 and $10 million.

While his projects were rising, his marriage to a college sweetheart fell, a casualty of Morris' total immersion in his business. "We grew in different directions," he says. Since then he's squired beautiful women to Sarasota night spots and on long weekends in New York and California—but at no cost to his civic interests. He is chairman of the Sarasota County planning commission and sits on a long list of boards and committees. When a local magazine recently listed the county's 12 most influential citizens, brown-bearded Robert Morris, 38, was there among the graybeards.

THE COMPUTER BUILDER

Two years ago, two of the founders of Ohio Scientific Inc., a manufacturer of home and small-business computers, sold their interest in the business for about $3 million in cash, making themselves instant millionaires before their 30th birthdays. Charity Cheiky, 29, and her husband Michael, 31, owe their fast fortune to a combination of her business talents and his electronic wizardry. Together, they developed and marketed the highly successful Challenger line of home computers.

Charity and Michael Cheiky (pronounced cheeky) met as undergraduates at Hiram College in Ohio, she in math and psychology, he in physics and chemistry. Shortly after graduation, they founded their company in partnership with Dale Driesbach, a Hiram professor, to make calculators that teach statistical concepts. That product flopped, but Michael, making use of newly mass-produced microprocessor chips, was ready with plans for a small, inexpensive computer. Charity aimed it at the hobbyist market, advertising first in computer magazines. Almost from the start orders rushed in. OSI products attracted computer buffs by offering them generous "functionality"—computing capacity—for the price. Later, the company developed higher-priced computers for small businesses.

In its first year, 1975, OSI sold $20,000 worth of computers. Sales in 1980 reached $20 million. As the company outgrew their ability to manage it, Charity and Michael commissioned consultants to screen corporate suitors. They finally accepted a bid from M/A-Com Inc., a business-communication systems manufacturer. The sale went through for more than $5 million; the Cheikys collected over half and Professor Driesbach got most of the rest.

Even after the young couple share the proceeds with the IRS, there should be enough to keep them in Jaguars and Porsches—their only extravagance. They are also staying on as OSI executives. But Charity, a shopkeeper's daughter, isn't at all complacent. Instinctively cautious, she says, "There's no such thing as financial security. Inflation could wipe us out if we don't invest wisely." With vision like that, Michael and Charity's financial future should be just great, thank you.

SMASHING OVERNIGHT SUCCESS

Celeste Yarnall became a star in real estate.

Twelve years ago Celeste Yarnall was an aspiring film actress who appeared occasionally with Elvis Presley or Robert Wagner on screen and regularly with a cast of thousands at the Santa Monica unemployment office. While still aiming for stardom, she was pushing 30 and figured it was time to get a real estate license. "I wanted a job I could do part time between movies or shows to pay the bills," says the former Miss Rheingold of 1964. Grubb & Ellis, a big Southern California real estate company, impressed by Yarnall's enterprise and good looks, hired her to sell commercial properties in Los Angeles. Soon acting was taking a back seat to selling office buildings.

Now a staff of eight financial analysts and commercial brokers work for her. Celeste Yarnall & Associates, founded four years ago, negotiated more than $53 million worth of leases and sales last year—one of the slackest periods in a decade for commercial leasing in Los Angeles. "In an overbuilt market, a good broker keeps busy finding fabulous deals in vacant offices," she says. "I got companies to move so they could get a year's free rent." Yarnall, 38, has exclusive leasing rights to such prestigious buildings as a 13-story tower on Sunset Boulevard that was designed by architect Charles Luckman. Her cut of the roughly $800,000 in commissions her company earned last year was $250,000.

Closing deals on the phone in her penthouse office in the Luckman building, she is as crisp as Joan Crawford. Says Yarnall: "The key to my business is being in touch at all times

194

with potential buyers and sellers, with tenants, landlords, architects and other brokers. I spend 30% of my time just talking to people with no particular deal in mind."

Off duty, though, you get the impression that she never really did abandon show business. Out on Wilshire Boulevard in her ivory-colored 1981 Rolls, with her press agent in the back seat, she cranks up the stereo volume on the soundtrack to *Flashdance* and bounces to the beat. This evening she hurries home to the red brick house in Beverly Hills she shares with her second husband and 12-year-old daughter to catch herself on the six o'clock TV news. Yarnall is the subject of a two-minute "new millionaire" profile. At its conclusion, she demands nervously of her publicist: "How did I do? How did I do?"

THE NUMISMATIC DEALER

"Specializing in ancient coins is like handling old masters: you have to be educated to deal in them." So says Bruce McNall, 30, owner of Numismatic Fine Arts, a Beverly Hills firm that dominates the enormously lucrative Greek and Roman coin market in the U.S. Commissions are the foundation of McNall's wealth, which amounts to somewhere between $30 and $50 million.

McNall holds master's degrees in ancient history from Oxford and UCLA. But he started his practical education with a boyhood stamp and coin collection. In a coin shop near his home town of Arcadia, Calif., he spotted a Roman coin from about A.D. 300 selling for 50¢. Buying it kindled a career. Off and on through his teens, McNall worked part time in coin stores, using his pay to acquire, coin by coin, 150 specimens minted by Roman emperors. By the time he was ready for college, in 1966, he had invested about $5,000 in his collection. Sotheby Parke Bernet then auctioned off part of it for $60,000. Says McNall: "One denarius of the Roman Emperor Trajan that I bought for $3.75 brought more than $300."

Besides putting him through college and graduate school in grand style, the profits from his hobby left McNall $30,000 to reinvest in coins and whetted his appetite for wealth. So he veered off the academic path in 1970 and took a job with a Los Angeles coin dealer.

Two years later McNall started his own firm, specializing in investment-grade coins. In 1973 he put out his first glossy catalogue and began a series of semiannual auctions that have helped establish his pre-eminence in the field.

Dealer commissions of 10% to 20% mount up fast on trades that sometimes run to millions of dollars; and with ancient coins appreciating 40% a year on average, growth seems assured. In 1980 McNall's firm had revenues of $30 million, earning its young proprietor $5 million before taxes. He also runs Summa Galleries, which sells other Greek and Roman antiquities and turned in a $3 million profit last year.

McNall, a bachelor, socializes with some of the super rich. His best customer lately has been Nelson Bunker Hunt, son of the late H.L. Hunt, the Texas oil billionaire.

SECURITY SUCCESS

Randy Brock runs a thriving army of security guards.

Like most shrewd cops, Randy Brock, 41, guards his thoughts, often concealing them behind a broad, even-toothed grin. But a moderate thickening at his midsection suggests that a career in private police work has been good to him. For most of its 13 years, his company, Brock International Security, has been one of the fastest-growing security services in the country. Its employees once guarded the Declaration of Independence and the Constitution and now watch over a number of Fortune 500 companies.

Brock's interest in protecting other people's property began at age 17, when he spent a summer tracking down missing books for the Philadelphia Public Library. "I found myself particularly suited to investigative work—all it really demanded of me was common sense," he recalls. After graduating from Middlebury College in Vermont, he was offered a commission in the Army and became a military policeman. He found the training invaluable. "Fort Dix was really a city of 45,000, and every crime that could happen happened," he says. He left the Army as a captain in 1970 and returned to his college town to set up a security business. The early years were downhill, but his military background eventually helped him get government contracts protecting the Philadelphia Naval Yards and the Department of Energy's nuclear project in Oak Ridge, Tenn. Last year Brock International Security, with 800 employees, took in revenues of 19 million, up 50% from 1981's $6 million.

Brock's runs his company somewhat like an Army D.I. For

198

example, he'll show up at a job at 3 a.m. to see that his guards are on duty and alert. "I convinced my men in the Army that I never slept," he recalls. But he's learned, the hard way, to delegate authority. When his company was still small, he put his name and number first on a roster of people for employees and customers to call 24 hours a day in case of serious problems. "The point came when I realized, 'Hey, wait a minute, my name should be last.'"

In five years Brock expects to be competing head on with Pinkerton and Burns, the giants of his industry. He just reached another goal recently months ahead of schedule: to amass a net worth of $1 million by the time he turns 40.

CRAFT PUBLISHING PROFITS

Kate and Rob Pulleyn publish three craft magazines.

Fellow weavers back in Albuquerque think he's commercial, and it's true in a way. Rob Pulleyn, 38, who now lives and works in Asheville, N.C., is more concerned with newsstand sales and reader surveys than with the condition of his loom. Nine years ago, he and his wife Kate, 34, started a newsletter for weavers; now, to their surprise, they find themselves tending a publishing company called Lark Communications that is worth more than a million dollars and employs a staff of 19. They put out three bimonthly craft magazines, the most successful of which, Handmade, has a circulation of more than 100,000. "We still have a sense of unease about the money involved," says Kate.

Their magazine careers sprang from a weaving supplies shop that opened in Albuquerque in 1974. Rob, who had amused himself in high school paradying the school paper, the Razor, with a broadsheet of his own called the Guillotine, decided to send a typewritten newsletter to his customers. It told them about local shows where they could display their work and also about new yarns and patterns. He called it Fibercrafts, and soon local weavers and spinners were filling its pages with homely advice. Before long the Pulleyns were charging subscribers $6 a year and, over objections of purist readers, having stories written by professionals, printing full-color illustrations on glossly paper and turning a four-page newsletter into a magazine.

In 1978, after moving to Asheville because they thought Albuquerque had got too big, the Pulleyns brought out a second magazine, Yarn Market News. Then in 1980 the Bonnier Group, a Swedish publisher, lent them $250,000 for their third and most ambitious publication, Handmade. It caters to sophisticated hobbyists who want to sew or knit sexy and fashionable clothes. Each $3.50 issue has patterns and pictures of about 40 garmets, and the Pulleyns are aiming for a circulation of 250,000 within two years.

Although most of the subscribers make at least $25,000, the three magazines have kept their homespun look. A number of local art teachers and crafters serve as editorial consultants, and the editors are more likely to solicit patterns from weavers in Missoula, Montana than from designers on New York's Seventh Avenue. Indeed, the Pulleyns readily take suggestions from just about anyone. "Our receptionist cast the decisive vote on which cover to go with on the last issue of Handmade," Rob admits.

The couple, who have a nine-year-old daughter, put in 60-to 70-hour weeks and pay themselves a relatively modest joint salary of $50,000. Perhaps because money has never meant a great deal to them, they are fearless in their readiness to expand their business. "The worst that could happen," Kate says, "is that we'd have to begin again from nothing."

MAIL-ORDER CATALOG MAN

Richard Thalheimer sells executive toys by catalogue.

Jogging through San Francisco's Golden Gate Park in April 1977, Richard Thalheimer took out his stopwatch—and something clicked. The watch was the kind that automatically calculates speed and mileage, and other runners often asked where to get one. Thalheimer, a lawyer, bought 25 of the timepieces at wholesale from a small manufacturer who said he could supply more if needed. The next step was to place a small ad in a runners' magazine. He sold 100 watches for a profit of $200—enough to whet his appetite. A second ad, for a more sophisticated and expensive wrist chronometer, produced 1,000 orders and $20,000 profit in only three weeks. Says Thalheimer: "I saw what everybody sees about the mail-order business—the chance to make a fortune overnight if you hit it right."

Today Thalheimer, 36, earns $250,000 a year as president at The Sharper Image, a mail-order house that specializes in luxury items for businessmen. A handsomely printed catalogue went to 17 million households last year and drew orders for $34 million worth of merchandise. He expects to reach an even larger audience through cable TV. Last year, on the nationwide Satellite Program Network, he launched *The Sharper Image Living Catalog,* essentially a 30-minute commercial that stars Thalheimer demonstrating his wares.

After his early success with the chronometer, Thalheimer read *How You Too Can Make at Least $1 Million (but Probably Much More) in the Mail Order Business* by Gerardo

Joffe (Harper & Row, $19.95). It taught him how to target potential customers and rent the best mailing lists for reaching them. With his line of "executive toys," as he calls them, he has outflanked even the economy. "People with money buy all year round and are not affected by recessions," he explains. They can splurge on a handmade replica of a medieval suit of armor for $2,505 or a $1,030 computerized fitness machine, but the average item is $125. The catalogue shrewdly mixes fantasy with function by blending technically detailed product descriptions and well-tempered hype.

A bachelor, Thalheimer has filled his office and $600,000 house with many of his products, including a $930 chair made from the bucket seat of a Porshe and a $225 battery-powered Baja racer that can go 30 mph. His success is a tribute to trendiness, but he denies having unusual ability to divine the public's mood. His rules for success: "Find something people want, advertise it in a small way, show a profit, then do it in a big way. Most people skip the two middle steps."

CUSTOMER'S WOMAN

Andrea Martin cooly keeps commodity profits growing.

Andrea Martin, 39, is among the highest-paid women brokers on Wall Street. As a vice president for investments at Shearson/American Express, she earned more than $200,000 last year.

Commodities and tax shelters are Martin's bread and butter; they command the highest commissions and attract the wealthiest clients. Her recommendations from among 18 Shearson-managed commodity funds earned her customers an average return of 60% last year.

The daughter of a wealthy Long Island couple, Martin started as a bookkeeper at a company near home and worked up to project manager for a California fiberboard manufacturer. In 1978 she began selling securities—mainly stocks—at John Muir & Co.

One mark of an outstanding broker is client loyalty. When Muir folded in 1981, Martin kept 90% of her clients by leading them and herself to safety just one month before the end. Sensing something amiss, she and a few other brokers had already transferred all the stock in their clients' accounts from Muir's "street" name to the investors' names. It was weeks or months before people with securities in Muir's name could sell them, but Martin's clients never lost control of their investments. Says she: "Switching the accounts was a nuisance, especially when I wasn't sure that the company was in trouble." But it helped her earn a reputation for defending her clients' interests.

Twice divorced, Martin lives on New York's Upper East Side but forsakes city sidewalks for Long Island bridle paths on most weekends. Horses are an investment as well as a passion. She owns a four-year-old thoroughbred, which she is raising for show. "It's the ideal hobby," she says. "I get a sport, a tax shelter and a chance to make a profit when I sell."

TUNED-IN TO SUCCESS

The Burnworths refine the pictures you see on TV.

Randy and Carolyn Burnworth send out the right signals—video signals, that is. They make equipment that enhances and refines the pictures produced by TV sets, video recorders and video cameras. The products look like stereo system components and are sold in electronics stores. Prices: $113 to $479. The couple own two related companies, both based in Tillamook, Oregon, about 60 miles west of Portland. Carolyn, 36, heads Showtime Video Ventures, which markets the equipment. Randy, 35, is president of Video Ventures, which develops new products. Last year he developed and she sold $3 million worth of components.

"Technology to me is the ability to make something simple," says Randy, a mechanical prodigy who reads 150 magazines a month and plasters the covers on the walls of the company lunchroom. One of the reasons Showtime does well is that its products are easy to operate. Another reason: they work. For instance, the Model 7000 audio-visual procesor ($449) plugs into a television set and improves the clarity of the picture. "We can make the best even better, absolutely blow you away," brags Randy, who calls himself an "imagineer." Video Review and Video magazines have tested and praised his products.

Burnworth decided to get in the video enhancement business when he became unhappy with the quality of his own home video. Before long, he turned his living room into a workshop and began reading books on enterpreneurship. His favorite: *How to Be Rich* by J. Paul Getty. Burnworth's business—and passion—until then had been building race cars, but he left autos for his specialized video field because "I saw that no one else was into it." Always eager to toot his own horn, Burnworth claims to have "personally invented" the still small industry of video-improvement products for the general customer.

While the Burnsworths put most of their profits back into their business, their joint $260,000 income pays for many pleasures. They recently built what they call an "outrageous" 13,000-square-foot, three-story house overlooking the Pacific Ocean. Cost: $290,000. The place boasts a dozen television sets, two with giant screens, and 13 video cassette recorders. The reception is enhanced, of course, with Showtime's equipment.

SPECIALIZED NEWSLETTER MAN

Llewellyn King sells high-priced news of energy and armaments.

Any newsman worth his expense account recognizes when he's onto a front-page story, but precious few recognize when a story is worth a whole new publication. In the early 1970s, before OPEC first flexed its muscle, Llewellyn King, a Washington newsman, sensed such a story: the looming struggle for energy. He realized further that no single publication was reporting it thoroughly. Says King, now 42: "There was a real need for coverage of the nuts and bolts of what was happening on all energy fronts."

In February 1973, King quit his job as Washington editor of McGraw-Hill's Nucleonics Week, scrounged up $250 and singlehandedly began publishing a newsletter on all facets of the subject. He called it the Weekly Energy Report and charged $250 for an annual subscription. Later that year a story broke with staggering worldwide implications: the Arab oil embargo. Suddenly, energy company executives, congressman, business consultants, sheiks, investors and others whose fortunes float on oil were eager to read every word Llewellyn King wrote.

Today the newsletter is called Energy Daily. A 13-member staff in Washington and three foreign correspondents serve approximately 2,000 highly attentive subscribers—at $800 for 250 issues a year. With similarly astute timing, two years ago King sired a second newsletter, Defense Week, that covers the Pentagon from all sides and angles. Almost 400 subscribers signed on the first year. Besides defense contractors and government officials, King thinks his readers include plenty of "spooks"—spies, that is. Of his first-year customers, a very high 85% have renewed their subscriptions—at $500 annually. King reckons the two letters as assets worth $2 million; his yearly salary is over $100,000.

A man of recognizable journalistic skills and personal flamboyance, King started chasing stories as a high school dropout in his native Rhodesia (now Zimbabwe). Wanderlust took him first to England, where he became one of the youngest correspondents on Fleet Street, and in 1963 to the U.S. He wangled work at the now-defunct New York Herald Tribune and later at Washington newspapers before joining McGraw-Hill.

As a leading spokesman of the energy industry, King is a popular lecturer. His rakish humor, insider's tales and sharp perception of business trends help him command fees as high as $4,000 a speech. With this added income, King buys fuel for two horses, a Lincoln Continental and a small plane.

THE MOVIE INVESTOR

Sheldon Starkman starred in his own cliffhanger—with a harrowing middle and a happy ending.

I'm a movie fan and I got addicted to the stock market," says Sheldon Starkman, explaining his curious accomplishment. He is a Los Angeles freelance artist who draws magazine ads and movie posters for a living. But for fun, he has been buying up—single-mindedly and staggeringly—shares of two major motion-picture companies, Warner Communications and 20th Century-Fox. Like many another virtuoso performance in Hollywood history, it sounds crazy but it worked.

When Denver oilman Marvin Davis bought Fox in June, company officials were astonished to discover that Starkman was Fox's largest individual shareholder. From an initial investment of $130 in 1974, he'd managed to pyramid his holdings to 48,080 shares in the company. That was worth $5.1 million after Davis' offer. Subtracting his enormous loans in his margin account, Starkman received $3.2 million from the Fox sale. (His Warner stock would net him over $1 million if he sold it.)

Starkman, 51, has stuck stoically with his investments, even when the stocks declined. To keep on buying, he borrowed heavily. "I was putting just about every cent I was earning into the stocks," he says. "Along the way I did everything but hock my house." To pay for all those shares in the two movie companies, he dug deeply into his $15,000-to-$30,000 annual income. He took out personal loans. When things were really tight, he even ate some of his meals free at an uncle's restaurant.

Over the years, he was able to borrow more than $2.3 million from the brokerage house that handled his trades. Much of his leverage came from increases in the value of his stocks. John P. Graner, manager of the Beverly Hills office of Bache Halsey Stuart Shields, where Starkman does his trading, analyzes his success this way: "He has a staying power that very few of us ever have."

In the early '70s, Starkman started sinking money in stocks in a modest way through his brother, Michael, a stockbroker. Since Starkman and wife Donna have no children and lead a quiet life, stocks became a hobby. Then something happened. One day in 1974, Starkman went to see *The Exorcist,* and he was thunderstruck by the crowds waiting outside the theater. The next day he called Michael and bought $1,000 worth of stock in Warner, which was distributing *The Exorcist.* Soon he began buying Fox too. He was impressed by a list of its upcoming films; he also felt that the stock was a good buy at $4.50 a share. Observes Michael Starkman: "Shel has always been a compulsive collector."

At first Warner rose from $10 a share to $18, but then plummeted to $7. All the way down, Starkman bought furiously. "I knew I was overextending myself," he says. "I was scrounging up money wherever I could." He did the same with Fox stock, which fluctuated between $4.50 and $9.50 a share throughout 1974. When both started to rise the following year, Starkman became completely mesmerized. He took to sitting in his bathrobe all morning, staring transfixed at his TV as stock quotations rolled across the screen.

In the six weeks after *Star Wars* came out—May and June 1977—he bought 4,900 shares of Fox at an average price of $22 each. Starkman spent $107,800 in all. But he wrote checks for just $15,187. Of that, he borrowed $5,000 from an uncle and $4,300 from a bank, withdrew $2,000 from his savings and took $3,887 from his income. The other $92,613 came from the increasing purchasing power in his margin account as the stock rose from $11 to $24.50.

The more valuable his holdings, the more he could borrow from Bache—and the more deeply he fell into debt. In 1978, he came within one day of a margin call, in which his broker would demand repayment of his outstanding loans, forcing him to sell at catastrophic losses. Fortunately, just then Chris Craft Inc. started buying Fox stock in an unsuccessful takeover attempt. That pushed the price back up, saving Starkman.

By early last year, Starkman had accumulated 32,535 shares of Fox. Then the stock split four for three. His equity had increased so much that he was able to relax a little. So he borrowed from his broker against his holdings in order to begin spending some money on himself. His major extravagance: a house in gilt-edged Bel Air on which he and Donna are spending $950,000. Admits Sheldon Starkman: "By all the laws of logic and probability, I was supposed to be wiped out. Instead, I'm rich."

RENTING THE SUN

Instead of selling solar energy, Billie Jolson rents it out.

If Billie Jolson, niece of the legendary singer Al Jolson, were given to song, she might belt out the showstopper from *Hair, Let the Sunshine In*. Over the past two years, the company she owns and heads, PEI (for Planned Energy International), has installed nearly $1 million worth of solar hotwater heating equipment. Most solar venturers have tried to get by on plumbing or mechanical skills. But Jolson is making good by her financial wits.

Her plan: to convert solar energy into an equipment-leasing tax shelter. Jolson, a CPA, devised limited partnerships that use investors' money to buy solar equipment and then lease it out. The partners get profits from rental fees, deductions for depreciation and additional income tax write-offs worth 25% of their capital—10% as a standard investment credit and 15% as a special credit for solar-energy backers.

PEI, in Newport Beach, Calif., leases the equipment—copper solar panels and plumbing gear—to heavy users of hot water, including hotels, restaurants and a coin-operated laundry chain. Through PEI, they can convert to solar energy without much cost or risk. Most customers are California firms. For example: Sun City Gardens Retirement Home near Palm Springs, which used to spend more than $6,000 a month to heat water electrically for its taps, swimming pool and spa, has reduced that bill by a third even after paying a $2,200 monthly leasing charge.

213

Jolson, an affable 48-year-old woman with two grown children, came by her financial knowledge during more than 20 years of selling real estate and managing the business affairs of movie and TV stars (Pat Boone, Roy Rogers, Andy Williams). Friends and business associates put up most of the $775,000 for her first two partnerships. The latest one, launched last month, is for $1.1 million.

As the general partner, PEI contributes 5% to 20% of the money. Jolson also plows back into the company some of the $72,000 a year that she earns as president. Her net worth is nearly $1 million, and her future value is tied to the success of the company—and solar energy. With deregulation of natural gas—the prime water-heating fuel—assured by mid-decade and perhaps as early as 1984, Jolson's forecast is sunny: "I'm going to have a nice big chunk of the solar market."

SHE TURNS ON THEIR LIGHT

Publisher Kathy Kolbe helps bright kids shine brighter.

Many a parent has joined a PTA committee and tried to improve the quality of education. Kathy Kolbe, 44, of Phoenix, did that—and more. She started an educational publishing company. Resources for the Gifted, that in only a few years has grown to sales of $1.1 million. Kolbe has gone from unpaid volunteer to $50,000-a-year president of her own firm. As sole stockholder, she could become a multimillionaire if she ever decides to sell out.

In childhood, Kolbe was handicapped by dyslexia and dysgraphia, which made her read and write backward. She overcame her problems with a vengeance. As she recalls, "I felt that if I could learn to write, I could be an author and if I could learn to read, I could be an editor." So she studied journalism at Northwestern.

Later, as the mother of two exceptionally bright children, Kolbe unintentionally launched her career in 1972 by complaining to the school principal about the lack of special programs for gifted kids—typically those with IQs of 130 or higher. That led to her being asked to chair a school district committee to develop such a program, and she spent a year interviewing parents, students, educators and psychologists. The paucity of special educational materials and the eagerness with which parents and teachers greeted her project helped to fan Kolbe's interest. To test her recommendations, in 1975 she set up a summer school for gifted children and founded Resources for the Gifted.

215

Fringe Benefit

After 5 years the school was so successful that Kolbe, with no formal training as an educator, started giving seminars on teaching the gifted child. Teachers deluged her with requests for classroom materials, and ads she placed in educational magazines and mailed to schools swelled orders. Kolbe's stock of books, games and kits from many publishers spread from a spare bedroom to three sheds in her backyard. She began developing, editing and publishing her own materials in 1979.

Resources for the Gifted has published 71 items designed to stimulate children's critical thinking, analytical reasoning and creativity. Through it all, making money has been almost a fringe benefit for Kolbe, who seems to derive her greatest satisfaction from her role as educational reformer. Doing well by doing good has brought her honors along with wealth: in April the Small Business Administration named her Arizona's small-business person of the year.

OLD GOLD

Imagine starting with $900 and within a year grossing over $600,000. Or taking $1,000, re-investing it five times, and walking away with $1 million four years later. If you think it's impossible, you don't know Steve Gabor's.

Steve, now 36, was just 9 prior to the Communist takeover in Hungary when he and his parents fled Budapest and immigrated to the States. His mother worked as a maid, his father as a factory worker making $1.10 an hour when they first arrived. "But my father told me never to work for anybody else," says Gabor. And Steve has been self-employed ever since.

He was 20 years old and in college when he opened his first store. "I was always interested in music," he recalls. "I spent a lot of time in record stores." So, he thought, why not own one? For Steve Gabor, this was a great idea.

Near his Los Angeles home Steve noticed a new discount record store called Aaron's Records. It was the first such store in Los Angeles and Steve was impresed with it. He went to the owner and asked for help in opening his own outlet. "I asked him how I could start my own place without any money," he laughs. "And the guy told me!"

In 1969 he "found a storefront near a school and around the corner from my girlfriend." Start-up costs were $900. He rented the store for just $200 a month without signing a lease. And since he couldn't afford a fancy sign, he parked his Volkswagen out front and mounted on his surfboard rack a sign that read, "Albums $2.99."

Volkswagen out front and mounted on his surfboard rack a sign that read, "Albums $2.99."

Next, he bought single copies of 200 albums from a local wholesaler. They cost him $2.49 apiece, so he made only 50 cents on each. But they sold, because all his competition except for Aaron's was selling the same albums for $2 more. Each morning Gabor returned to the wholesaler and replaced the albums he'd sold the day before, and by the end of the first month he was grossing close to $15,000.

The real key to his success from the very beginning, however, was his ability to float cash. Once he could show that his store would do a certain amount of business, he was able to establish credit and increase his inventory. His credit rating also allowed him to open four new stores in the next six months. By year's end he was averaging $60,000 a month per store, which he immediately reinvested in more records or other business ventures.

"That was when the record business was fun," Gabor says with a smile. "There was no competition. All the record companies were independent and you could cut your own deals with them. You could fight them down from $2.40 to $2 a record. And you were a big shot if you did $1 million a year. Today the business has gotten much more sophisticated. Record companies are conglomerates and you have to make a $10 million a year to be a big shot."

The changes in the record industry of course brought change to Gabor's business, but he didn't let that throw him. He sold all his stores but one, the Music Odyssey, which he still operates. Instead of concentrating solely on discount records, he turned the Odyssey into a "youth-oriented super-market." He began selling used records and "paraphernalia." T-shirts, buttons, bumper stickers and smoking accessories came first. In 1972 he installed a pinball arcade in the store's mezzanine. And he tapped into the newborn video industry. "We sell and rent videocassettes. All ratings, G to triple X," Gabor says.

When he realized videocassettes could be rented he began renting records as well, and later added 25 video games to the pinball machines on the second floor. Gradually he built up the business. Today its grossing $1.5 million a year.

By 1975, says Gabor, "1 was burnt out. I was working at the store seven days a week, 12 hours a day. I figured there had to be an easier way to make money." So he went back to school and got his real estate license. Then, using the same principle of floating his cash, he put down $1,000 on spec for a condominium in the fashionable Southern California community of Pacific Palisades. He guessed that the three-story townhouse would take longer to build than the three months he'd been promised, and he was right.

Construction took over a year. And by the time the condo had been completed it had risen $20,000 in value. Gabor sold it at that profit without ever having fully paid for it. He then repeated the process in five different locations, including Hawaii and San Francisco. Four years later that $1,000 had mushroomed into $1 million. Gabor took the million and bought Music Odyssey, the land it was on, and the four-story apartment building behind it from his landlord.

"I come up with a concept and act on it," says Gabor. "You can't be afraid to move." Following his own advice,

Gabor has been "in and out of a dozen businesses in the past 12 years." Whenever he had profits from his record store, he'd plow them into new businesses, most of which were intentionally short-term ventures.

"I used to come up with a concept a day," he says. "Now I've slowed down to one a week."

Find a Need and Fill It

To Gabor, business is simple. "You start because you see a need. Then you fill it, using courtesy, good product and good service as your key tools."

Gabor points to his policy at Music Odyssey. He has chosen his inventory so "there's something for everyone who walks through the door. If they walk out without buying, something's wrong, and we go after them to find out what it is. When was the last time a salesperson promised he'd provide exactly what you wanted? That's what we try to do."

One of the essential factors in Gabor's operation, of course, is the people who help him run it. He realizes that. "The same key people have been with me for 10 years," he says. "I appreciate them and I pay them well. In return, I've found them to be very loyal."

Gabor still runs all his businesses as he did his first: close to the line. But he's changed his general approach somewhat. "I believe that the most important rule is also an old Chinese proverb," he says smiling, "Work smart, not hard."

FASHIONABLE
ENTREPRENEUR

At the ripe old age of 14, Lucy Mackall got her first taste of what foreign competition can do to a small-business person. She was all set to make paper flowers and sell them to stores when she realized that she couldn't possibly undersell the Mexican imports. She gave up on that project, but 20 years later she's found the success she used to dream about as a kid. Most people would be doing well to have one business going, but she's got three. Together they'll gross over $4 million in 1983, not bad for a woman who started with not much more than her own two hands and a knack for coming up with winning ideas.

Mackall spent her childhood in Greenwich, Connecticut, and her university days at Wheaton College, from which she graduated in 1969. For 5 years after that she built architectural models for a leading firm in Boston. One day in 1974 a friend called and asked if she wanted to become partners in a retail store. "I though about it carefully for 2 seconds and said yes," recalls Mackall.

The partnership went down the tube, but Mackall's career in the retail trade was off and running after she moved herself across the street to an empty storefront. Her first challenge was figuring out what to sell. She eventually settled on brightly colored tote bags—there were other tote bags on the market, but virtually all of them were on the drab side. Business was good and costs were low, mostly because Mackall did all the sewing herself. Still, it wasn't until she opened up a second store in Boston's well-known Faneuil Hall Marketplace that the operation really took off. The increased exposure helped

Mackall do $200,000 worth of business the first year at the new location; she paid back the $3,000 she had borrowed from her folks out of the first week's receipts. Now that one store grosses a cool half-million dollars a year, and she's got four other Lucy's Canvas shops besides (plus a factory where the bags are made).

That mini-chain would be enough to keep most people busy, but not Mackall. In 1977 she opened a shop called Have-A-Heart, which Mackall says was the first one in the country to specialize in products with a heart motif. The stock ranges from mugs and glasses to stationery and clothing, but all the items have one thing in common—hearts, either painted on or incorporated into the item's shape. Initially Mackall had to scour all sorts of shops to assemble her inventory, picking up one item here another there. As the fad caught on, she was able to arrange for manufacturers to produce merchandise directly for her store. She was also able to expand her operation by selling franchises; currently she has 10 of them scattered across the country. Another indication of her success was the striking number of nearly identical shops that popped up in various locations. If imitation is the sincerest form of flattery, then Lucy Mackall certainly has a lot of admirers.

But Mackall still wasn't finished making her mark. In later 1979 she was at a trade show looking for grommets and other supplies she needed for her canvas-bag business. There she ran into an exhibitor who had a machine that could put images on shoelaces. She ordered some laces with hearts on them, figuring they'd be a natural for her shops, and she started wholesaling them as well. But the turning point came at the National Stationery Show in 1981. "People just went nuts over the laces," recalls Mackall. "In 1 month, our peak, sales were over $1 million." By the end of the year she had shipped four million pairs to over 6,500 outlets in the U.S., Europe, Japan and South Africa. Business has slackened somewhat recently, but it's not due to a lack of variety: The laces come adorned not only with hearts but also with frogs, unicorns, sailboats, rainbows, ice cream cones and many others as well.

Mackall isn't always right, there have been a few losers along the way. For example, she once tried to sell her canvas bags and heart merchandise by mail order. "It was a disaster," she says. "The catalog was hard to read, and it didn't reach enough people or the right people."

Over the past 10 years she's been in business, Mackall has developed a real dislike for the "wheeler-dealer" type of individual. "I'm very honest and can't stand liars," she states firmly. "That has sometimes been a problem in my business dealings, but I'm a lot less naive now than I was before."

Mackall plays almost as hard as she works, spending her time windsurfing, running and playing tennis. All in all, she's living proof that people who get moving get ahead.

THE INSURANCE MAN

Running all the way, Lynn Hutchings has turned on arid corner of Wyoming into green.

Wyoming life insurance man Lynn Hutchings is driven to succeed—at whatever he does. His boss and friend, Sam Clark, who supervises the Farm Bureau Insurance Co. agents in western Wyoming, is fond of telling stories about Hutchings, his super-star. "Two years ago, when Lynn took up running, he told me he just wanted to get a wittle exercise," Clark recalls. "I said, 'Lynn, you may be able to con some people, but you're not fooling your best friend. I'll bet that within a year you'll be running marathons.''

Sure enough, a year ago Hutchings was able to finish the 26.2-mile Las Vegas marathon in 3:43, an enviable time for a beginner. He still runs 60 to 70 miles a week, and hopes to better his Las Vegas time in the St. George marathon in Utah.

Hutchings' whole life is run at the flat-out pace of a man training for a long-distance race. That's the main reason why, at 33, he is one of the nation's most successful insurance salesmen. For nine straight years he has been his company's best agent, and this year he will sell life insurance with a face value of $35 million, plus lesser amounts of health and property coverage. From it all, his income will be more than $250,000. Most striking, Hutchings has accomplished all that from a one-man office in Rock Springs, a dusty Wyoming town of 25,000.

His father cooked, his mother waited on tables, and there was little income as Hutchings grew up in Evanston, Wyoming. After high school, he sold auto parts for several years, then met a Farm Bureau Co. supervisor, who he impressed as a potential insurance salesman. It took a while to persuade the company to hire an untried 22-year-old. But the Farm Bureau finally assigned Hutchings to Rock Springs. "At the time," he recalls, "we had no business there at all, so maybe they sent me in because there was nothing I could screw up."

Far from stumbling, he has done so well that he now insures more than 20% of the town's population. His clients are mostly blue-collar workers and ranchers. "I relate to them because I don't have a college background," Hutchings says.

Hard work has been his best policy. His prodigious week begins at 5:30 Sunday afternoon with four to five hours of phone calls to line up appointments. In the following five days (it used to be six), he works 60 hours or more (that used to be closer to 70), visiting as many as six present or prospective customers each day. Hutchings doesn't stop to eat, nor does he take clients out for a drink or a meal. "People tend to be frightened of me because I'm so intense," he concedes. "But from a business standpoint, that also gives them confidence in me." Consequently, 33% of his phone calls and an astonishing 90% of his personal visits result in sales.

The payoffs are visible: a 10-room house in Rock Springs; a $200,000 second home in the Teton Mountains of northwestern Wyoming; two Oldsmobile Toronados, an $18,000 Corvette and a Ford; and a Bellanca Turbo Viking airplane, which Hutchings pilots to speaking engagements before insurance groups and on vacations. The $75,000 plane is one of

Hutchings' most satisfying rewards.

There have been penalties too. Says he: "When I came into insurance I knew I wanted to be extremely successful, and I was willing to pay the price." His first marriage broke up in 1972 and, Hutchings says, "I almost lost my second family two years ago. I just hadn't taken the time to know them or let them know me." To save his marriage, he agreed to trim his workweek and spend more time with wife Chris, 30, and their two young daughters.

Hutchings feels he has begun to relax a bit, but he's wary of letting up too much. "I have this continuing sensation that the bubble's going to burst," he says, "because I'm not really any different from anyone else—I just work harder." Yet in the estimation of his boss, Sam Clark, that drive itself distinguishes Hutchings from other people. "Insurance men get an awful lot of negative response," Clark observes. "But when Lynn gets his nose bloodied, he isn't discouraged. He just keeps on charging."

THE HERB MERCHANT

As a boy, Morris ("Mo") Siegel visualized he'd become a millionaire by the time he was 25. Somewhat to his disappointment, he says, "it didn't happen until the second week I was 26." Nor did it happen until he'd gone through a 1960s hippie phase. Capitalizing on that experience, though, Siegel grabbed a fmont seat on the health-foodbbandwagon and proved himself a champion drum-beater for herb teas. His eight-year-old company, Celestial Seasonings in Boulder, Colo., earned $800,000 last year on sales of $16 million, and Siegel, 33, is worth a soothing $4.5 million.

In 1970 Siegel recruited his wife Peggy and a friend, Wyck Hay, to help him comb the Colorado hills for the ingredients of an herb tea they called Mo's 24. They sold the caffeine-free concoction to a local health-food store. A year later, Hay's brother John joined them, kicking in $800. That winter, Siegel drove to New York City and back, calling on health-food stores that had started sprouting all over the country. He sold them Mo's 24 and primed them for his upcoming Red Zinger, a mix of rose hips, hibiscus, lemon grass, peppermint, orange peel and wild-cherry bark.

Siegel is a marketing genius. He gave some of his teas funky names such as Grandma's Tummy Mint and Morning Thunder, and he festooned the packages with Disneyish artwork and campy homilies ("Angels can fly because they take themselves lightly"). When John Denver, Colorado's state troubador, was host of the *Tonight Show,* he got a guest to plug Red Zinger. In 1972, Erewhon, a Boston distributor of natural foods, took on Celestial's line, and Siegel managed to get his teas on the shelves of some large supermarket chains.

In the beginning, Celestial was a laid-back operation; job applicants were asked about their attitude toward truth, beauty and goodness. When Siegel wanted to scrap that philosophy, John Hay balked. After a few fractious years, Siegel prevailed. He then hired experienced executives so that he could concentrate on long-range projects, such as an herb "coffee" due out in February. Though he still sees himself as outside the corporate establishment, he mutes his flower-child image by wearing a sports coat—or even a three-piece suit.

DAVID SARNOFF
FATHER OF TELEVISION

In the first half of the 20th Century, Russia and the Union of Soviet Socialist Republics lost three outstanding people to the United States. One of them fled the Soviets, leaving behind most of his material possessions which were seized with the Communist takeover of Russia. His name was Sergei Rachmanaoff, the well known composer, pianist and conductor. Another was a philosopher-novelist who was later to launch a major intellectual attack on all forms of collectivism, and have a profound influence changing the way people think in the Free World. Her name was Ayn Rand., author of "Atlas Shrugged" and other blockbuster philosophical novels. The third person was only a boy who emigrated to America with his family in 1900, seeking the promise of the "Golden Land." His family was only one among the many thousands who were looking for a new opportunity in the "Land of Promise." Later in life, the young lad of nine years age was to be dubbed the "Father of Television"; his name was David Sarnoff.

It had taken David's father four years to save enough money to buy steerage for his family to make the trip.

David had been sent to live with his uncle, when he was five years old, to begin Talmudic studies. For the next four years, in next to poverty conditions, he was to acquire the virtues of patience, concentration, and a good memory that would serve him well in the American business world.

Arriving in America, the young Sarnoff boy of nine and one half realized that the "promise" in the "Promised

229

Land" was something to be earned; it wasn't free. Some of the pennies from his sales of Jewish newspapers were soon to mean the difference between eating and not eating for his family. Due to his father's failing health, he was soon to become the major bread-winner for his family.

David learned to speak English somewhat fluently within his first year and read whatever books he could get his hands on. He had to sell fifty newspapers each day to make a profit and soon built his first route. He built a makeshift wagon and increased his sales by selling to newsstands. His business eventually won him the prize of getting his newspapers first ahead of the other boys, so that he then started selling at a discount to other delivery boys. Still making a profit, this gave him more free time. His next perception was that if he could only buy a newstand, the problem of paying the rent and feeding his family was solved.

After searching ads, he came upon a bargain. $200.00 would buy just the newsstand he had been looking for. But the $200.00 was so much beyond his reach that it looked all but impossible. News of his efforts to support his family and his desire to buy the newsstand had spread around the neighborhood. A total stranger greeted him one night as he returned home. It was a pleasant middle-aged woman who had heard about his plight. After questioning him about his education, his family, and his goals, she handed $200.00 to David. He forgot to ask her name and address but never forgot her face and did not learn until 20 years later that the money had come from her boss, a wealthy man who chose to remain anonymous. David, two decades later, was to have this same woman help others through his own anonymous gifts, thereby repaying the gift he had received. Although David Sarnoff was only thirteen years old at the time, his family was able to move to a larger flat near the newsstand. It did not matter that the new location was in the heart of Hell's Kitchen in Manhattan.

Now that his father had become a total invalid, David knew that he would not be able to go on to high school upon graduation from elementary school—he had to look for a "real" man's job. But this would not mean the end of learning for him. Temporary poverty was unfortunate; ignorance would be disgraceful. Like many newsboys, David wanted to become a reporter. Deciding to apply for work at the New York "Herald," he accidently went in the wrong door and found himself in the office of the Commercial Cable Co. The noise of telegraph keys clicking had a strange attraction to him and he got his first job as a messenger-boy. This "accident" was later to have far reaching effects on his life and spread his name around the world.

The world of telegraphy fascinated him from the first day. Names such as London, Tokyo, and Paris responding to the fingers of a telegraph operator was a whole new world. He immediately saved enough money to buy a dummy telegraph key and a Morse Code book. Along with practicing on the key, he also studied books on electricity and telegraphy. Soon, during more quiet hours in the telegraph office, some of the operators would let him send and receive messages.

He would hold his job as messenger boy only until the Jewish High Holidays. His was the soprano voice in the choir and when he told his boss that he must sing in the choir, he was fired from his first full time job.

There had been another telegraph operator working in another office and David had made friends with him over the wires. He went to see the man personally for the first time. Jack Irwin told him that there might be an opening for a junior operator at the Marconi office. George De Sousa, who would play a part in David's life for many years to come, hired him as an office boy at $5.50 per week. The date, September 30, 1906, was to become commemorative for many years in one of America's largest and most adventurous corporations—RCA; the Radio Corporation of America. Years later, David Sarnoff would state that the electron was discovered in the same year he was born. He would also state that in 1906, when he joined the Marconi Wireless Telegraph Company of America, that he had made his contact with the electron.

In December of 1901, the airwaves across the Atlantic Ocean were breached for the first time by Guglielmo Marconi; the first "wireless" message had been transmitted and received. The year 1901 also witnessed the first transmission of the human voice via "wireless" and Reginald Fessenden was able five years later to perform the same achievement, but not only within his laboratory walls—operators on ships at sea were startled to hear a woman singing through their earphones, although they had been listening for dots and dashes.

By 1904 wireless telegraph stations were popping up on the world's coastlines. In January of 1907, Lee DeForrest applied for a patent on the first vacuum tube, his Audion tube as he dubbed it. Though wireless activities were being promoted by various companies, most of them floundered. The American branch of the English Marconi Company was the most re-

232

nowned even though it was the largest wireless company. Marconi equipment had been installed on only four ships and four land stations; it was at one of these stations that David Sarnoff had taken the job as office boy.

David took seriously his new opportunity; now he was in a business that reached around the world. He absorbed whatever technical knowledge he could and made it his business to acquire the positive traits of character from the men he worked under. In 1906, David met Marconi personally for the first time, and from him acquired a new vista of the progress of electronics and science.

Because of the inspiration of Marconi, the second portrait hung on his office wall next to the immortal Lincoln would be that of Marconi himself. These two portraits would continue to hang across from his desk as he moved into positions of larger and larger responsibility.

Within one year David was promoted to his first position as telegraph operator at a salary of $7.50 per week. He had just turned sixteen.

A new opportunity soon followed when a ship operator became ill just before sailing on the S.S. New York. David assumed his post and crossed the Atlantic Ocean for the second time, but this time not in a foul steerage hole. He was a ship's officer with a private cabin and a glamorous uniform. His reputation as the fastest and clearest telegraph operator was beginning to grow.

Returning to land duty, he assumed various positions as operator until 1909 when he was made manager at the Sea

Gate, Coney Island station, the busiest station and the nearest to New York City.

In 1911, opportunity at sea again appeared. A sealing fleet had been persuaded to test the Marconi equipment and David went along as one of the operators. On two occasions David was to partake in sending medical information via wireless on the voyage. One occasion was credited with saving a man's life. This was the first time wireless was used for medicinal purposes, and the Marine Medico Service regards its origin in David Sarnoff's first efforts. The sealing company purchased the Marconi equipment which was David's first sale for the Marconi Company.

The year 1912 was also to mark a major event in David's life. A new 5KW station had been installed above the New York Wanamaker department store to promote sales. David Sarnoff became operator and manager of the station. Although the public in general was still largely indifferent to the new phenomena of "radio" (which by 1912 had replaced the term "wireless") there were those who worked in the new industry who understood its future greatness.

In April, 1912, the indifference would change to alarm. On April 14, David received the message; "SS Titanic ran into iceberg. Sinking fast."

The calm-shattering message had come from the SS Olympic which was 1,400 miles away. The well publicized maiden voyage of the Titanic, which was the fastest, most luxurious passenger ship of that time, and its impending catastrophe drew the attention of the world. The President of the United States even ordered all other stations except the Wanamaker station to close down so that news could be clearly received of surviving Titanic passengers.

The airwaves had become jammed by transmissions from other stations and vessels at sea. For three days and nights Sarnoff remained at his station to report his receptions to a shocked world. 1,500 people perished and hundreds more than the 750 survivors could have been saved if other ships in the area had been equipped with radio.

With the passage of the Congressional "Radio Act," the Marconi Company flourished; ships with more than 50 passengers were now required to be equipped with radio. Since United Wireless, its only larger competitor had gone bankrupt, Marconi now dominated the industry.

David was first promoted to radio inspector of installations on ships, a few months later to inspector for the whole country and finally to traffic manager. He also became an instructor at the Marconi institute, to meet the new urgent demand for radio operatiors.

In 1914, newly elected vice-president and general manager Edward Nally realized that he needed someone to oversee the sale and installation of all Marconi equipment—David Sarnoff was promoted to contract manager.

Radio was next tried successfully on railroad trains, with Sarnoff riding along at the key.

The "feedback" or "regenerative circuit" (grid amplification) invented by Edwin Armstrong was demonstrated at Columbia College for Sarnoff and two Marconi engineers. Messages were picked up from as far away as Ireland and Hawaii. Sarnoff called the Armstrong invention "the most remarkable receiving system in existence." Company officials did not receive Sarnoff's report on the Armstrong amplifier gratefully since it would require new investment and obsolescence of existing equipment. Years later, they would purchase the Armstrong device for much more money than they could have bought it then.

1914 was also a very happy year for David's family. One evening, after gathering his family together (with the exception of his father, who had died a few years earlier), David informed his mother and the others that they were moving. There was one catch; they were to leave everything behind, including the furniture, dishes, linens, etc. Their new home was to be in a nice part of the Bronx and have electric lights, a bath, hot water and steam heat; all of which were considered luxuries. The new home would be completely decorated and stocked.

Making himself aware of the rapid developments and inventions in the electronic industry, David Sarnoff realized that the Marconi Company must take advantage of all advances to stay in stride. Sarnoff memoranda began to flow to his superiors. These were his first attempts to steer not only his company but the entire industry as well.

David Sarnoff understood the new science of electronics. He would later be called its "prophet" because of the many predicitons he made which materialized. He was not a major innovator, nor could he be classed even as an inventor. He was a business administrator par-excellence because he could see the potentials of the new science and press for their realization. In 1915, in another Sarnoff memoranda, he was beginning to write of the common household radio or "Radio Music Box" as he termed it. However, radio would have to wait until the early 1920s. The First World War was well on its way and demands would change sharply.

In late 1916, David Sarnoff testified in Congressional hearings for the support of private enterprise dominance in the new science of radio and electronics. Some Washington officials using the war "emergency" were proposing that the government should take over radio. This was to be only the beginning of David's many and varied efforts in support of private enterprise and human freedom. In this case as secretary for the Institute of Radio Engineers, he was speaking for an entire industry.

However, when the United States entered the war, the discussion came to an end; the government took control of all high-power stations including Marconi stations.

As of January 1917, the Marconi Co. promoted David to the office of commercial manager; the company had reorganized its efforts and wanted to bring a number of departments together for greater efficiency. He was now in charge of over 700 people and the installations of nearly 600 sea vessels. He negotiated all contracts and supervised government and private customer sales. The Marconi Company now revolved around the Commercial Department and Sarnoff managed it.

Disasters and wars have a record of accelerating progress of invention and technology and World War I was no exception. When the Titanic sank ocean going radio became a must. When the Kaiser's U-boats cut British under water cables, radio took their place. Demand for radio supplies reached new peaks and Marconi sales exceeded the $5,000,000 mark in 1917. Marconi equipment was used on airplanes for the first time.

Another important feature resulting from the war was the growing desire for American dominance in the new radio industry. The Alexanderson high-frequency alternator was believed to be the best of existing methods for sending electromagnetic signals. Among the big electric companies, General Electric had control of the alternator. Since the Marconi Company (American) had become the leader in its field, it was considered to be the key in the formation of a new company to establish American prominence. GE representatives went to England and negotiated the purchase of the American branch of the Marconi Company. The new company was to be the old Marconi Company (American branch) with major ownership and control vested in General Electric. Owen D. Young, an official at G.E. and a lawyer specializing in high finance was to be the new chairman of the board. George DeSousa (who gave David Sarnoff his first job as office boy at Marconi) was named treasurer, and E. F. W. Alexanderson (inventor of the high-frequency alternator) was named chief engineer. David Sarnoff was to continue as manager of the Commercial Department. On December 1, 1919, the new company began its existence. It was to be named the Radio Corporation of America—later to be known everywhere as RCA!

Under the new arrangement, GE was to do all the manufacturing for the two companies while RCA would handle all marketing and communications services. Each had access to the other's patents through a cross-licensing agreement. Not more than 20% of the stock could be owned by foreign interests. Two months after the formation of RCA, the government returned ownership and control of all stations back to the original owners. Patent piracy, dispute, and litigation abounded. Among the electric companies, none had a clear dominance of inventions to take advantage of integrating all the advances thereby enabling it to offer a superior service. Westinghouse Electric had by now purchased the "feedback" inventions of Armstrong and also controlled other patents of high importance. Among the various companies including wire companies such as AT&T there was no less than a "patent stalemate." In middle 1921, the GE-RCA patent and licensing pool would be expanded to a GE-RCA-Westinghouse pool. Westinghouse would be awarded 40% of production with GE retaining 60%.

Immediately with the formation of RCA, David Sarnoff was recognized for having superior knowledge and vision in the field of radio.

With the foundation laid for a major push forward, David Sarnoff began in January of 1920 to revive his desire for the "Radio Music Box" he had proposed in 1915. Other companies such as the United Fruit Company had been drawn into the patent-licensing consortium to form a new Radio Group. To prevent anti-trust litigation by the government, federal officials had been made aware of all contracts negotiated to create the Radio Group. Internal communications of global radiotelegraph services with RCA leading the way among the group led to the construciton of a ten acre installation at Rocky Point, Long Island, which was to be known as "Radio Central." The first giant antenna was powered by a series of new 200-KW Alexanderson alter-

239

nators. The President of the United States, Warren G. Harding, threw the switch that started Radio Central's operations, and delivered the first message on the new system. He was heard in Europe, Hawaii, Japan and Latin America. Modern broadcasting was born.

1912 was the beginning of the home made "crystal set." Invented by U.S. Army General Henry H. C. Dunwoody and developed further by others, the device became a national craze. In 1915, David Sarnoff had proposed a "Radio Music Box" with simple controlled station selectivity. No one had yet thought of using advertising to pay for the cost of broadcasting. Income was viewed as coming only from the sale of equipment. Amateurs had been buying parts and building their own receiving sets. One "ham," who was an employee at Westinghouse, had built a transmitter at home and started broadcasting music in his Pittsburgh neighborhood. Dr. Frank Conrad, the broadcastor, started receiving requests for different musical selections, and his licensed signal 8-XK became well known in the area. Pittsburgh stores noted an increase in sales of phonograph records. Producers of phonograph equipment had feared the advent of radio because they believed it would lessen their sales. The opposite was taking place. Conrad's audience grew and a local supplier of radio parts decided to use the station to advertise. Conrad had moved his station to the top of the Westinghouse plant and was reaching larger numbers of people; the advertiser sold out his entire stock and people scrambled to nearby cities to buy up more parts.

When news of the events reached executives of the Radio Group, they became much more responsive to David Sarnoff's proposal for a new "Radio Music Box." The world's first true broadcasting station, KDKA, began operations on November 4, Election Day. The presidential election returns were broadcast for the first time and the novelty created an even greater demand for electrical accessories. Eight months later, on July 2, 1921, at the urging of Sarnoff, the heavyweight championship fight between Jack Dempsey and Georges Carpentier was also broadcast. The event was reported in the American and European press as the world's first real broadcast.

Sarnoff never had a controlling interest in RCA stock nor was he to become chairman of the board for years to come. This meant that every move he wanted RCA to make was subject to the approval of stockholders, the board of directors, and various committees. It is significant that the Technical Committee would only allow $2,000.00 for the development of "Radiola," as the new Radio Music Box would be called. The RCA technical staff had suggested an amount ranging from $10,000 to $20,000. The following table demonstrates the results of Sarnoff's projections of January 1920:

		Projected	Results
1st year	(100,000 Radiolas)	$7,500,000	$11,000,000
2nd year	(300,000 Radiolas)	22,000,000	22,500,000
3rd year	(600,000 Radiolas)	45,000,000	50,000,000
		$75,000,000	$83,500,000

In 1929, RCA would gross $176,500,000 with a net profit of $15,800,000 on this investment.

Automobiles, telephones, and home lighting had come slowly to America. Radio bloomed rapidly. 32 stations were licensed in 1921; 254 in 1922! The names of performers and newscasters soon became household words.

In 1921, Sarnoff's salary was raised to $15,000 annually. In May of that year he was promoted to General Manager; four months later, vice-presidency was added to his title. Radio was rapidly becoming a household necessity.

From the beginning of the formation of RCA, David Sarnoff let it be known to everyone that his goal was complete independence for RCA. He viewed the existing structure as limiting to RCA's potential since RCA was only allowed to function in the areas of sales and service. GE and Westinghouse took care of manufacturing. New companies like Zenith and Philco were much more flexible due to incorporation of all functions under one roof. RCA was rapidly outgrowing its restricted original role. The rapid changes in style, prices, techniques, and production in the industry demanded flexibility. Because of David's insistence on research, RCA was constantly innovating. His belief in general access to patents led to a rival company's reaping great profits. In fact, RCA was lagging its rivals in the sale of radio sets.

In 1924, RCA again took the lead when it introduced the superheterodyne principle invented by Edward Armstrong. RCA had paid Armstrong $200,000 cash and awarded him a total of 80,000 shares for his superregenerative and superheterodyne principles. Armstrong became a millionaire overnight! It should be noted that the superheterodyne principle is employed in all radio sets even today.

David saw radio reaching even the most humble home and bringing all forms of culture to it. As early as 1928, Sarnoff was projecting "sight communication as promised by television"—a generation ahead of its time. Based on an examination of Armstrong's experiments in 1920, Sarnoff told of the coming use of short wave radio for commercial purposes; at least seven years ahead of its time. In 1922 he said that automobiles would be equipped with radios and a year later that "everything that moves or floats will be equipped with radios." Even hand held or portable "radiolettes" were a near reality in his perspective. David Sarnoff was beginning to gain the reputation as a "prophet" for an entire industry. Increasingly, from 1923 onward, he talked of the coming commonplace of television. One of the most foreboding projections he presented was a comment made in 1926 that "a future war may last five minutes rather than five years, and yet be infinitely more destructive."

Sarnoff's imagination was serving as pace setter for an entire industry. Another Sarnoff characteristic was his approach to problems; he always tried to see the long term benefit in each problem. The prolonged charges of monopoly, lodged by others against RCA, had led to antitrust invesitgations and time consuming litigation. Eventually it would all lead to independence for RCA, the withdrawal of the telephone and electric interests from broadcasting, and the formation of NBC—the National Broadcasting Company. He also encouraged competition in broadcasting and in 1922 spoke of an American Broadcasting Company; he believed the competition would enhance the quality of programming.

It is worth noting in this context that the telephone interests were not losers, but gained considerably; RCA was destined to be their biggest customer, with a bill of $15,000,000 in the late 1960s! Also, ABC, formed soon after NBC, would surpass NBC in revenues and profits by the mid 1930s.

In the early 20s, companies such as Western Electric and American Telephone had been experimenting with various methods of adding sound to motion pictures. In contrast to the sound-on-disc method being tried, General Electric was developing a sound-on-film approach. Profits to the motion picture companies were running high and they were even hostile to the addition of sound to silent films.

"The Jazz Singer" starring Al Jolson made its debut on August 6, 1926, and revolutionized the industry. Produced at a cost of $100,000 the "talkie" grossed millions. Warner Brothers, using the Western Electric disc method, had stolen the day.

However, David Sarnoff had believed all along that anywhere the reproduction of sound was a possibility, this was an opportunity for RCA. General Electric, sensing the superior capabilities of RCA research, retired from the field. RCA, in conjunction with Paramount Pictures, released the highly successful "Wings" in 1927; the sound was recorded on a separate film and run simultaneously with the picture film. The RCA "Photophone" method got its real impetus when Sarnoff, in collaboration with Joseph Kennedy (President John F. Kennedy's father) formed RKO (Radio-Keith-Orpheum) Pictures and produced a series of Hollywood's most profitable films.

As early as 1921, David Sarnoff had attempted to combine the radio and phonograph into one unit, or "under one roof" as he termed. He approached the Victor Talking Machine Company first, but officials at Victor would not agree to the radio-phonograph merger. Then entering into an agreement with the Brunswick Company, the initial order for radio receivers was around $1,500,000; public acceptance more than matched David's projections and the radio-phonograph sysem was born. Finally, in 1925, the Victor Talking Machine Company stockholders sold out to RCA and the now famous "listening dog" logo appeared. "His Master's Voice" became the "RCA Victor" slogan; even though the RCA Victor Company would not be a real entity until December 26, 1929.

In 1929 Sarnoff was promoted to executive vice president of RCA and also asked to take part in the reparations talks with Germany. J. P. Morgan, the financier, was among his associates on the trip to Europe and the two men were to form a lasting friendship before returning to America.

The stock market crash did not hurt Sarnoff directly. Using the same logical processes that he used in radio business, he foresaw the market overvaluation and had sold the shares of various stocks he owned just a few months before the crash. He was to repeat the process in the 1931-1932 market and the profits he made enabled him to live well during the depression years.

In January of 1930, Owen Young resigned as chairman of the board of RCA. General Harbard moved from president to chairman and David Sarnoff was elected president of RCA. Sarnoff was now age 38.

On May 31, 1930, the justice department filed suit against the members of the radio-telephone group which included RCA, GE, American Telephone, Westinghouse and their subsidiaries. "Monopoly" charges had become old news to Sarnoff by now. Since RCA was only doing 20% of radio set business, the "restraint of trade" allegation appeared ridiculous; the company had actually advanced trade and others were reaping profits in the lucrative industry. The suit was to drag on for nearly three years; out of it Sarnoff was again to grasp the opportunity. Two days before the trial, a consent decree was reached; RCA would now become a separate entity with full corporate capacity, including manufacturing. The terms involved a variety of licensing agreements, royalty payments and stock swaps, but RCA could now go its own way. Sarnoff was later to remark that "The Department of Justice handed me a lemon and I made lemonade out of it." This type of bravado was typical for him since he did not view healthy self-esteem as a fault.

From the high of $16 million in profits in 1929, RCA had dropped to $796,000 by 1931. Sarnoff ordered economies in all departments in the company (including his own salary cut from $80,000 to $51,000) except in the department of research. He insisted that their business was "obsolescence" and that research was the foundation of the growth of RCA.

Sarnoff was opposed to most of the New Deal policies of Franklin Roosevelt, who was elected president in 1932, and he made no bones about letting everyone know it. He also let it be known that he classed Soviet Russia in the same category with Nazi Germany.

Vladimir Zworykin is to television what Marconi was to

radio. Although Campbell Swinton had theorized, in 1911, that the Braun cathode tap could be used for electronic scanning, it was in 1923 that Zworykin applied for a patent for his "iconoscope"; later to be dubbed the cathode ray tube. He joined RCA in 1929 and a demonstration was made at the Institute of Radio Engineers. Industry leaders and the press ignored it, yet history was being made. The first TV transmitter was operated on top of an RCA Victor plant. In 1932, a telecasting station installed on top of the Empire State Bulding brought much more encouraging results. All modifications of either the television transmitter or receiver required a modification of the entire system since it functioned as a unity. Microsecond errors in synchronization would completely distort images on the CRT. The number of scanning lines was raised to create better images. In 1935 Sarnoff raised the issue of "an experimental program" which meant that the "how" of telecasting could be accomplished was becoming an issue of "what" would be telecast.

Even though other companies had been conducting television experiments, RCA was well in the lead. On October 20, 1938, addressing members of the Radio Manufacturers Association, Sarnoff declared television to be technically feasible in the home and stated that RCA and NBC would demonstrate a limited commercial telecasting service to coincide with the opening of the New York World's Fair in April, 1939. "Now we add sight to sound," declared Sarnoff at the system's presentation. The first regular telecasting programs were begun within days with the selling of receivers priced at $625.00. April 20, the first day of public broadcasting, would later mark the day of the beginning of TV broadcasting and to Sarnoff would be applied the appellation, "father of television."

All issues relating to television had to wait for a number of years, however. World War II had begun and the entire electronics industry would be devoted to winning the war. Sarnoff also played a number of key roles in the war effort. Prior to D-Day, the invasion of Europe, it was recognized that communications was an unintegrated jungle. The mass of equipment made by different manufacturers coupled with the separate and uncooperating national networks demanded an expert to straighten it all out. Sarnoff was assigned the rank of colonel and ordered to England to serve as special assistant to General Dwight D. Eisenhower, Allied Supreme Commander. The Allied Forces Network was made functional in time for the invasion, even though Sarnoff personally had to resort to going to Winston Churchill to accomplish it. With the liberation of France, he was sent to Paris to organize communications in that country as well. Eventually, his efforts in the war would elevate him to the rank of Brigadier General; later, in civilian life, the "General" would usually be used with his name.

The devastation that he observed in Europe stuck with him and his future "predictions" would always be modified by the necessity for the world to solve its social and political problems. RCA had already launched its first guided missiles before the beginning of World War II and Sarnoff was well aware of the potential of atomic energy before the first bomb was dropped on Hiroshima. He was fully aware of the potential negative uses of radio and television. Years ahead of its time, he urged that a "Voice of America" be created to counter the totalitarian propaganda being generated in countries such as Nazi Germany and Communist Russia.

Returning to civilian duty at the end of the war, he faced

the problems confronting the promotion of television. By late 1946 RCA would be producing a limited number of TV transmitters and receivers. The general public was very excited at the prospects of television. The radio and electronic industry was another story. TV channel allotments could almost be had for the asking. Industry faith in television was so low that CBS only purchased one of the five licenses assigned to it; years later it would pay millions to retrieve those same licenses. NBC willingly purchased all ten licenses assigned to its two networks.

RCA had staked $50,000,000 on television under Sarnoff's leadership. Now that investment would flow back in abundance. The number of sets produced by the company in 1946 was around 160,000. Four years later, the company produced a total of 7,000,000.

Until 1950, NBC television operated in the red. Two years later, all losses were recovered and profits grew on a cumulative basis. By now, Sarnoff considered television to be the greatest victory of his life so far.

Television up to this point was a monochrome, or one color, system. The next move was the introduction of color TV. Controversy had grown over whether to use the mechanical (whirling-disc) or electronic method. CBS was promoting the mechanical system; RCA was advocating the electronic. Either system had to have the approval of the FCC to be sold to the public. The mechanical method was obviously superior in image quality and color tone. The electronic method needed much improvement as any observer could see. If the electronic method could be perfected it would be indisputably superior to the mechanical because a person with a monochrome set could watch a color broadcast even though he would not see it in color. The mechanical system would require separate broadcasting and receiving systems. The electronic system was, in other words, "compatible" to either monochrome or color broadcasting and receiving.

By October, 1950, there were 8,000,000 TV sets in use and an audience of around 30 million people. Decision in favor of the mechanical system would mean that anyone wanting color, or even to see programs broadcast in color, would have to purchase another TV set. RCA had continued to perfect the electronic method while the FCC hearings were conducted. Before the FCC decree, RCA made a public demonstration of its improved electronic method. It obviously matched the mechanical method and still had unlimited capacity for further improvement. In spite of the improvement plus the known "incompatible" handicap of the mechanical method, the FCC approved the mechanical system.

General Sarnoff announced that RCA would not accept the FCC decision and that they would continue to develop the electronic method. He also announced that RCA would file suit and take the issue to the Supreme Court if necessary.

On December 20, 1950, the Federal District Court ruled against RCA. On May 28, 1951, the U.S. Supreme Court did likewise. What is pertinent in the case is that the higher courts considered only the legality of the issue and not the substance. However, Sarnoff would not accept the fact that an appointed government agency had the right to issue such a decree, without the challenge of reviewing the substance of a case. He has been attacking this aspect of Big Government ever since. But the story does not end here.

An ad hoc panel of TV manufacturers issued a report in favor of RCA color only one month later. Soon thereafter, CBS broadcated a gala premiere of its new mechanical system. There was only one problem. Even though there were over 8,000,000 sets in use, hardly anyone watched the program. To view it they needed a special adaptor. The press was not silent, and attacked the CBS mechanical system from all quarters.

Months rolled by and CBS failed to produce any new mechanical sets. RCA, in the meantime, continued to develop the electronic system and shortly after the CBS premiere, a public demonstration was made; viewers with monochrome sets were able to watch the color broadcast in black and white. In addition, RCA color quality was still better.

As the months rolled by, CBS still failed to capitalize on its legal advantage; company officials were beginning to realize that the mechanical system was an economic impossibility. Three years later, after its momentous decision, the FCC, on December 17, 1953, reversed itself and approved the RCA electronic method. Sarnoff had won again. The electronic system is used throughout the world even today.

RCA had invested $130 million in color television before making the first dollar in profit. The first color TV sets retailed for $1,000; they were produced at a loss. Only 5,000 sets were sold in 1954 after the FCC reversal. Then, in 1955, sales volume jumped to 120,000 when set prices were sharply reduced. It was not until 1959 that the first profitable year was reached but by 1961 color television had become a $100 million business. Four years later it reached the $1,000,000,000 (one billion) status.

Other companies that entered color TV manufacturing purchased RCA picture tubes because of their superior quality.

Hardly had Sarnoff won the electronic/mechanical battle when he took up a new one—color broadcasting. NBC was the main provider of color programs for years. By 1966, 95 percent of its regular evening shows were in color. Although ABC had continued to increase its color programming through the years, it was not until 1965 that CBS made a serious attempt to offer extensive color programming.

Eventually one of David's son's, Robert Sarnoff, was elected to president and chief executive of NBC. The network was to prosper greatly under his command. To this very day, NBC still continues to lead the other networks in news programming.

The magnetic tape used in television, the electronic light amplifier, and the all-electronic air-conditioner are also RCA creations. They were all created ahead of schedules set by Sarnoff.

Not all of Sarnoff's projections were realized but enough of them have become realities to elevate him to the human elite. What his life has demonstrated is that the American Dream is not a fantasy. The rags-to-riches potential has not lessened but increased because of the abundance of opportunities that present day progress offers.

The computer revolution has already created new millionaires in America. Beginning in 1984, television reception direct to the home from satellites orbiting the earth will become a reality. The home telephone can now be used as a link-up between the home computer and distant computer banks for different information. Perhaps the roof-top satellite antennae will be used for home computers in the same way.

"Always and everywhere freedom and science flourish best in the same climate, each fortifying the other," Sarnoff stated in 1953. "It is this difference of approach, believe me, that will determine whether 'your course' will be just a treadmill—or a fascinating highway... It will not be a chore but an adventure if you bring to it a sense of the glory of striving—if your sights are set far above the merely secure and mediocre." Surely, these words do not come from a man empty of content. The life of David Sarnoff support them.

BIBLIOGRAPHY

"The Very, Very Rich and How They Got That Way" — Max Gunther

"Creative Mind and Success," "This Thing Called Life," This Thing Called You" — Ernest Holmes

"Think and Grow Rich," "The Law of Success," "How To Raise Your Own Salary," "Success Through A Positive Mental Attitude" (with W. Clement Stone) — Napoleon Hill

"The Magic of Thinking Big" — David Joseph Schwartz

"The Fabulous Greeks" — Doris Lilly

"The Secret Place of the Most High," "Love Announces Itself" — Jackson Fink

"Grinding It Out" — Ray Kroc

"The Gospel of Wealth" — Andrew Carnegie

RECOMMENDED READING

"Anthem," "The Fountainhead," "Atlas Shrugged" — Ayn Rand

"Human Action," "Bureaucracy," "Planning For Freedom" — Ludwig von Mises